Blue Lyra Review
Volume III

MATTHEW E. SILVERMAN, Managing Editor & Publisher
ADRIENNE ROSS SCANLAN, Nonfiction Editor
NANCY NAOMI CARLSON, Translations Editor
LAURA HONG, Web Editor
LENORE WEISS, Copy Editor

ISSN: 2167-8243

Cover Art: **X-Magritte**, 2012 by Nick Veasey

DEDICATION

BLR would like to thank the amazing dedicated staff who all volunteer out of love for editing and literature. We also thank you the readers and writers who help support the wonderful voices, both online and in print.

BLR would also like to encourage you to donate to a charity. Outside the arts, *BLR* makes donations to:

- **The Jewish National Fund** to help plant trees in Israel (http://www.jnf.org/),
- **The Red Cross** (https://www.redcross.org/),
- **The Fruit Tree Planting Foundation** to help plant fruit in poor areas so it can benefit both the planet and provide nutrition (http://www.ftpf.org/),
- **World Wildlife Fund** or the **WWF** (http://www.worldwildlife.org/).

volume 3

CONTEST WINNERS

FICTION

NONFICTION

POETRY

TRANSLATION

Fabienne Josaphat is a writer living in Miami. Originally from Haiti, her work is mostly centered on the native land and its people. Her previous publications include *Off the Coast Poetry Journal*, *Grist Journal*, *Fourth Genre*, *Damselfly* and *The Feminist Wire*. Her novel, *Dancing in the Baron's Shadow*, has recently been slated for publication in Spring 2016 with Unnamed Press.

Bookshelf

The thing my father was most proud of was
his bookshelf. Not for the density of oak
rippling its age across the side finish,
or the cubby holes like rectangular mouths
waiting to swallow stories stocked throughout
his years of hunger and thirst for words.
The thing my father was most proud of
was his bookshelf because on it
were his books, half-read and at first glance placated
in silence, mute as a lineup of a hundred convicts
crushed against the wall of their own offenses,
facing the execution squad, before curious minds
fire questions at their upright spines:
why was Mohammad Ali pressed beside Alex Haley?
And what could Sankara possibly have to say to
Sekou Touré? What secrets of state could they cough
up? Their whispers stir up the dust of historical
hysteria, revealing the undoing of leaders gone mad,
of writers' delirium, of novels written in darkness,
and then of books of codes decrypted for law,
penal and civil, bound in coarse, hardened leather,
stilts for my father to stand on and crane
his neck with pride, his beak a pair of shears
cutting my brain open. One day, he hopes
I will need the shelf, hopes I will take the books
in my hands and wipe their covers clean,
and look beyond the binding.

Hair Poem

That needle scratch, that lick on vinyl,
that banjo strum tonight—
that high-pitch screech we hear
is that of my hair
under the metal teeth
of afro picks, and my mother
thumbing its chords like a kalimba.

Taming wilderness is serious business,
and with a dip of her finger
in the *mascreti* butter,
she glides the jelly,
smooth and easy,
along the strands of hair.
She tries again.
The comb bites the knots,
rakes down the part.
Now the terrazzo beneath
our feet is blanketed
with kernels of coiled peppercorns,
failed resistance against the metal jaws.

Her fingers jive now, rhumba,
cha-cha with the section:
it's how she twines and weaves
and domesticates that thing.
One day, I say, one day
I will have my mother's hair,
Soft & Beautiful, Dark & Lovely,
manageably straight. Meanwhile,
she says, pick up that dispersed herd,
those fallen feathers of your flock
and toss them in this fire
so that they burn and shrivel down
to an oily pulp, so that we may stir
this tar again in the amber oil
of that jar, regrow and recycle
what's come out, preserve its Goliath strength.

J. P. Dancing Bear is editor for the *American Poetry Journal* and Dream Horse Press. Bear also hosts the weekly hour-long poetry show, Out of Our Minds, on public station, KKUP and available as podcasts. He is the author of thirteen collections of poetry, his latest book is *Love is a Burning Building* (FutureCycle Press, 2014). His work has appeared or will shortly in *American Literary Review*, the *2014 Poet's Market* and elsewhere.

Nevada, 1963

Do you remember your pre-war? How a part of you thought
with a fashionable dress and shoes you could almost forget
the way we once turned sand into glass. You ignored
the desert all around you, thinking enough water would grow
anything back, but you got scrub brush and shadows
for your beliefs. Did you really leave the baby carriage
out in the burning sun just past earshot, in case
your only child woke up in the uncomfortable brightness?
                    •
I remember your yellow dress almost as the sun. I remember
playing with scorpions while you were waiting for something
to take root in the Nevada sand, waiting for my father to return
a better man. When I see you even now, I see you watching
the horizon, where all suns touch the desert, and that old house
fills with hot silence right before everything disintegrates.

Tim Seibles, born in Philadelphia in 1955, is the author of several poetry collections including *Hurdy-Gurdy, Hammerlock*, and *Buffalo Head Solos*. His first book, *Body Moves*, (1988) has just been re-released by Carnegie Mellon U. Press as part of their Contemporary Classics series. His latest, *Fast Animal*, was one of five poetry finalists for the 2012 National Book Award. In 2013 he received the Pen Oakland Josephine Miles Award for poetry and he received the Theodore Roethke Memorial Poetry Award for Fast Animal, given triennially for a collection of poems. His poetry is featured in several anthologies; among them are: *Rainbow Darkness*; *The Manthology*; *Autumn House Contemporary American Poetry*; *Black Nature*; *Evensong*; *Villanelles*; and *Sunken Garden Poetry*. His poem "Allison Wolff" was included in Best American Poetry 2010 and, most recently, his poem "Sotto Voce: Othello, Unplugged" was featured in Best American Poetry 2013. He has been a workshop leader for Cave Canem, a writer's retreat for African American poets, and for the Hurston/Wright Foundation, another organization dedicated to developing black writers. Tim is visiting faculty at the Stonecoast MFA in Writing Program sponsored by the University of Southern Maine. He lives in Norfolk, Virginia, where he is a member of the English and MFA in writing faculty at Old Dominion University.

Morning Where You Are

"Don't go around looking like I would if I could
but if I can how can I"
--Mom

Some spring days
she and her sister, Eva,
strolled up Boyer Street,
and you could tell

they were *The Bluford Girls*
again—blue suits, black heels,
gold pins—and early April
pulled up in its cool limousine.

I was a teenager then
and had no idea what
that walk meant: the royalty
in it, the defiance— how

in what seemed a few years,

what could never end
would end: my aunt dies
on a bad mattress,

one flat soda in the fridge

and my mother, stolen
from herself, her smile
no longer made
for her mouth.

Maybe now   it's always sunlight
splintered behind the trees: evening,
the wind down. Cars,

like conversations, pause
and move on—my mind walking
its three-legged dog

from this   to that
and once more, I begin
to think about Barbara Bluford,

English teacher, pinochle player
born on a train bound for Virginia:

my mother grew up a city girl,
proud of her father, the one
black dental surgeon in Philadelphia.

When I was little, I'd sit on her lap
and wave from the window: *my* father
waving back, headed for the bus.

It was the early 60s: the news
just beginning to bleed.

She was kind and solid in that
take-no-nonsense parental way
and dressed so sharp

that a glimpse might cut'cha.
Those hats she wore to church:
bronze feathers blazing against gold

or the rose crown with the cream band
braided around a brim so wide
it held another sky.

*

Some nights we played *Pokeno*.
Four glasses, grape Kool-Aid:

me, my brother, and my Dad.
She filleted the cards
like a 5-star chef.

The kitchen clock adding up,
the tiny jackpot ripening.

*

My mother swears she's never cooked
a turkey; though for five decades,
she did it twice a year. Last Wednesday,
she started pouring *Wheaties*
at sunset. I was on the phone,

"It's evening, ma—*evening*."
She said, "It may not be morning

where *you* are, but it's
morning *here*."

Before the bad dentures,
she had the gladdest smile—

a morning unto itself:
any day starting over
wherever she found us.

"In college,"
my father said,
"she used to smile
like that   *at me*."

When she slipped in the lecture hall
he picked her up— Fisk University,
September 1945:

WWII barely over, fall-out still flying the stratosphere.
Lamp lit nights, my father below her window,
his Kappas to her Deltas—the brothers in chorus,

his hopeful solo climbing the ivy   *Only you…*

                  *

    Picture the lit major
    in Arna Bontemps' English class: her mid-calf skirt,
    her blouse, blue jay blue, the matching pumps,
    hand up, the answer a lantern in her eyes—

    and Mr. Chemistry, *Thomas Seibles, III*—
    dapper cat from Oklahoma, snap-brim hat,
    pin-stripe suit, spit-shined shoes, that easy
    side-to-side shuttle of his shoulders when he walked:

                  *

my nearly adult parents, beautiful—
their bodies still brand new.

On the honeymoon, Niagara Falls
must've flashed over them like an avalanche:

a passion like sunrise that first time,
like meeting a Prophet and having all
the answers asked.

Growing up, I thought
I knew   what was what,
the hammer of each day

barely missing me, *me*
with my mother's face,
my father's heavy hands.

I remember:

    Les McCann jammin' the living room—
    Dad, cool on the couch, patting his thigh.

      Mom's fearless soprano on Sundays,
      those butter rum *Lifesavers* on the subway.

    TS on his tie clip,
    The story of that five-pound bass.

So this is what

what   turns into—bits
of your life straggling
behind you—empty cans
hitched to the newlyweds' car

or the ragged tail of one red kite,
my father playing it
like a big fish in the sky,

and my mother
brushing my *brillo* head,
teaching me the wonderful
"cinnamon toast" and how
to act in church

and not to wear polka-dots
with plaids.

Erin Redfern's poetry has appeared in *Zyzzyva, Compose*, and *Scapegoat Review*. She has been nominated for Best of the Net 2015 by *Crab Fat Literary Magazine* and *Blue Lyra Review*. In 2015 she served as poetry judge for the San Francisco USD's Arts Festival and as associate editor of *Caesura*. www.erinredfern.net

Boom Box

Remember how many batteries a beach trip took?
I could sling the strap of my bubblegum pink
boom box and carry it like a purse.
Two decks to make mix tapes, but mostly
I used it when something good came on the radio,
not even looking up from homework spread
out on the carpet, recording over last week's
hits until the cellophane strip was a palimpsest
of pop voices and Top Gun guitar riffs.
Remember how good we got at guessing
when to stop rewinding so we could hear
that song from the beginning, that A side single
someone bought the whole tape for? There's no
such thing as fast-forward anymore, no time
for hyphenation. So that when I find a stack
of old calendars, the looped scrawl is a stranger's.
Who was this girl who scheduled driver's ed classes
and summer league games, who slipped
her slim sense of self into relationships
like tape decks, pretending the B-side songs
could be as good, wanting to be belted out
like arena rock, listening only for a backbeat
she could dance to, as though synched motion
were commensurate with being understood?

Laura Cesarco Eglin (author) was born in Montevideo, Uruguay in 1976. She is the author of three collections of poetry, Llamar al agua por su nombre (Mouthfeel Press, 2010), Sastrería (Yaugurú, 2011), and Los brazos del saguaro (Yaugurú, 2015). Cesarco Eglin's poems and translations have appeared or are forthcoming in a variety of journals, including *Modern Poetry in Translation, MiPOesias, Eleven Eleven, Puerto del Sol, The Acentos Review, Columbia Poetry Review, Timber, Pilgrimage, Periódico de Poesía, Metrópolis*, and more. Her poems are also featured in the Uruguayan women's section of Palabras Errantes, Plusamérica: Latin American Literature in Translation. Cesarco Eglin's poetry will appear in América invertida: An Anthology of Younger Uruguayan Poets (Ed. Jesse Lee Kercheval) forthcoming from the University of New Mexico Press in 2016. Cesarco Eglin holds a BA and an MA in English from The Hebrew University of Jerusalem, and an MFA in Bilingual Creative Writing from the University of Texas at El Paso.

Jesse Lee Kercheval (co-translator) is the author of 14 books including the poetry collections *Cinema Muto*, which won the Crab Orchard Open Selection Award, *Dog Angel* (University of Pittsburgh Press), *World as Dictionary* (Carnegie Mellon University Press) and bilingual Spanish/English poetry collection *Extranjera/ Stranger* (Yaugarú). Her translations of the Uruguayan poet Circe Maia have appeared in such magazines as *The New Yorker, the Boston Review* and *American Poetry Review*. The University of Pittsburgh Press will publish *Invisible Bridge/ El puente invisible: Selected Poems of Circe Maia* in August, 2015. She is also the editor of *América invertida: an anthology of younger Uruguayan Poets* which is forthcoming from the University of New Mexico Press. She is the Zona Gale Professor of English and Director of the Program in Creative Writing at the University of Wisconsin-Madison.

Catherine Jagoe (co-translators) is a writer and translator specializing in Spanish and Catalan. She has a PhD in Spanish literature from the University of Cambridge. Originally from the UK, she now lives in Madison, Wisconsin. Her translations include the Amnesty International award-winning Argentine novel *My Name is Light* by Elsa Osorio (Bloomsbury, 2003) and *That Bringas Woman* by the nineteenth-century Spanish novelist Benito Pérez Galdós (Everyman, 1996).

Mourning by Fainting

At times I wake up
and I'm already dizzy; I close
my eyes again
and rewind the film on foot
knowing there's nothing
the blood doesn't know; nothing
that doesn't waver
even continuity is
intermittent; certainty can be jolted
the wall is cracked
from floor to ceiling in a wave of crazy zig-zags

the stairs sway, go up slowly—fast
go down sideways; forced landing
gravity distributed in all directions
my hands try to break my fall; the throbbing
I feel in my eardrums was
in my heart not long ago

A una vigilia del desmayo

A veces despierto
y ya estoy mareada; cierro
los ojos nuevamente
y rebobino la película a pie
entendiendo que no hay nada
que la sangre no sepa; que no
hay nada que no titile
hasta lo continuo es
intermitente; una sacudida vacila la certeza
del piso al techo está la pared
rajada en una ola de peldaños entretenidos
agitando los escalones a subir despacio —rápido
a bajar al costado; aterrizaje forzoso
la gravedad distribuida en todas las direcciones
van las manos para atajar; el bombeo
que siento en el tímpano estaba
en el corazón hasta hace poco

Tentacles

The embrace of the jellyfish in February is the only one
in 243 straight days. The arms of an abacus
stay parallel. It's easier to mark
in colors the days in the past that sum up
the hours to stress that jellyfish is not
adequate for something that gives
such intimate contact, the mark
of the meeting burns
on the arms and legs the sand
the living sea shuns me.

Tentáculos

El abrazo del aguaviva de febrero es el único
en 243 días contados. Los brazos de un ábaco
se mantienen paralelos. Es más fácil calificar
en colores los días pasados se resumen
las horas de ir a recalcar que malagua no
es adecuado para alguien que da
un contacto tan íntimo, arde
la huella del encuentro
en los brazos y las piernas la arena
me aleja el mar vivo.

Cassie Pruyn is a New Orleans-based poet born and raised in Portland, Maine. She holds an MFA from the Bennington Writing Seminars. Her poems and reviews can be found in *AGNI Online*, *ENTROPY*, and *The Double Dealer*, with work forthcoming from *The Normal School* and *32 Poems*. She was a finalist in the 2013 and 2014 William Faulkner-William Wisdom Creative Writing Competition, and a finalist in the 2013 Indiana Review 1/2K Prize.

Flaneur on Royal Street, New Orleans

A hot Sunday in August.
Men sprinkle the ditches
with buckets full of sawdust,

shoving their brooms grittily
through the narrow, balconied streets.
The potted vines hang swaying in sleep.

The shutters, door-length, stay shut.
I want to leave to go visit her, but I don't;
occasionally when I call, she picks up.

Why love a river more than a woman?
An actual river, or the memory of one.
(I map out the valleys; I follow the sun.)

This street cuts a narrow trench of houses,
lively with bird calls––bunching,
dispersing. I could get on a bus,

or a plane, or a train,
show up on her doorstep, half-hidden in rain,
or speckled in snow, as I've imagined

I might. What would I say?
I'm sorry, Or
It was you who taught me how to stay away.

On the Hudson, years ago, I collected pamphlets
on the town's history, the Tivoli riots,
squatting among the one-room library's stacks,

or made sketches of sumac and sycamore,
beauty berry, box-bush––I can't remember––
every now and then looking around for her

and pretending I wasn't.
It was over by then. We were barely friends.

But in those days, she was the Hudson.

Back then, if I saw her walking
past my porch on Saturday mornings
in her green jacket, I'd call out, *Good morning!*

willing her to stop in.
Today, I gaze up at the wire-lines,
pondering communication again.

This city's only business is the constant reminding
of the murky Mississippi's winding,
and the river's revenge, and the river's conspiring––

Enough about rivers! Remember the night she called
just before they took her liver out, when I cried
Let me come! but it wasn't the time,

and they hooked her by the ribs like a stripped fish,
and excised the swollen, black-blotted flesh,
meanwhile I rallied friends, east to west,

and begged them to pray, or whatever else,
and instead obsessed
over sending her flowers....

Now the sky darkens to mottled mess;
across the river, rain falls in sheets;
I run to the car before it keels over––

No more adventures on a glacial river.
No more daffodils and Volvo bombers.
Today, no more thinking of her,

only the rain as it twitches and leaps.
Why love a river more than a woman?
The river distracts me from grief.

Judy Bolton-Fasman has completed a memoir entitled *The Ninety Day Wonder* from which this essay is based. Her work has appeared in the *New York Times, Salon, The Rumpus, Brevity, 1966: A Journal of Creative Non-fiction, Cognoscenti* and other venues. Her website is www.judyboltonfasman.com.

Calle Mercéd 20

I often dreamed in Cuban.

It didn't matter that *me rompie los dientes*—I broke my teeth—if I tried to express a complicated thought in Spanish. I spoke a kitchen Spanish in which my accent was intact, but my fluency came and went. The fact that I understood Spanish so well relegated me to the role of observer early on. When I lived in New York after college, I'd listen to the Latina girls on the subway chat each other up about boys and clothes and the nightclubs they went to on Saturday nights.

Beyond the kitchen, I rarely gave myself away as a Latina. Like my Sephardic forebears, it's in my blood to be secretive that way. My Cuban mother and her children came together to worship in song and dance like the crypto-Jews once did in Spain. But Beny Moré was our God. We climbed Beny's—*montaña querida*—his beloved mountain where his *guajira* lived. I daresay we were *guajiros* too. We lived in our own private village where we turned up the hi-fi to spin ourselves into star-flecked dizziness. My mother, though, danced with one hand on her stomach, the other hand raised in the air as if she were taking an oath. Her dancing intimate as it was, embarrassed me.

My father's family, the American Boltons, said that my Cuban family were peasants. The Alboukreks, my mother's family, said that the Boltons had *los narizes en el aire*—their noses in the rarefied air of New Haven, Connecticut. I think that Grandma and Grandpa worried that we favored my mother over my father. What would Grandma say if she saw us orbiting like blue and red marbled planets around my mother, a golden sun with sharp rays?

Dad, on the other hand, threw open the curtains and also turned up the hi-fi. My mother said he had that kind of confidence because he was born in America. She had a fantasy that if she had been born here she could dance in the open with her children.

We followed Dad into the broad daylight of his fervent patriotism. My sister, brother and I were a ragtag army of three that he marched to the music of John Philip Sousa. We exchanged Beny's trademark seagull squawk at the end of *Soy Campesino* for the trilling piccolos threading Sousa's booming, declarative *Stars and Stripes Forever*.

**

Cuban-American. American-Jew. Cuban-Jew. Juban. Sepharic-Ashkenazic Jew. Yiddish-Ladino speaking Jew. I am the product of a mixed marriage of sorts who has ended up as a Temple-going, non-praying, selectively kosher, non-fasting, skeptical, superstitious, terrified, brazen, monotheistic, mezuzah-kissing, idol-worshipping Jew. I sat on the hyphens that strung together these identities. I pumped higher and higher on each of them like I once did on the wheezing swing set in our backyard.

The Spanish that is slipping away from me is also hyphenated. It is a Spanish that has come to rest somewhere between my mother's rapid-fire fluency and the drawn out a's and e's of Dad's Americano stilted Spanish—a language that he picked up on his trips to Central America and Cuba.

I went to Cuba in November of 2012 to look for my mother's landmarks, but Dad's spirit was also with me. The Havana I saw was an aerosoled city. *Viva la Revolución* was spray painted everywhere. The Cuba that Dad visited before 1959 was a sexy, rum-soaked playground for the Mafia and spies alike. Castro changed all of that when he came down from the Sierra Maestra Mountains—another *montaña querida*—and triumphantly marched into Havana on New Year's Day 1959. My mother, who once waved the Cuban flag for Castro, angered my father when she said that some of Castro's reforms were good for Cuba. Dad constantly reminded her how the dictator had bamboozled the Cuban people. Castro alone was responsible for the Alboukreks fleeing the island with 90 percent of the country's middle class.

Calle Mercéd 20 in Old Havana was the storied address of my childhood. All things Cuban began there. It was Never, Never Land, the place of my mother's eternal youth, the house that my grandparents left after living there for 40 years. When I finally saw Calle Mercéd I knocked on number 20's heavy wood door. That same door Abuelo stumbled in after a night of drinking away his paycheck. That same door my mother gently tapped to let Abuela know she was home.

A young pregnant woman answered the door. She lived in the apartment with her husband and extended family. She let me in and I walked into a living room overwhelmed with maroon brocade furniture and a big screen television on without the sound. After all of my mother's stories about living in luxury, I was surprised that the space was so small and that there were no marble steps. My mother made them up along with the maid that shined them.

However, I immediately recognized the open-air courtyard between the dining room and the kitchen. Sometimes Abuela brought home a live chicken and called the *shochet*—the kosher butcher—to slaughter the animal for the Sabbath meal. I imagine him cutting the chicken's throat in that space between cooking and eating. As I walked the length of the courtyard, I looked up to see laundry hanging from a balcony like team pennants.

I also visited the Havana synagogue— *El Patronato* Jewish Center—where my mother grew up. Women in the balcony, men gathered below around the raised *bima* just like the sanctuary in the Spanish-Portuguese synagogue in New York City where my parents finally married. But I was more interested in *El Patronato*. As my parents' original wedding invitation announced, their *ceremonia nupcial* would have taken place there in December of 1959 if my father had not left my mother at the altar for that first wedding.

I hadn't realized that the Jewish Center was built only in the 1950s. Other than the hotel where I was staying, it was the most modern of all the buildings I saw on that trip. *El Patronato* had a ramp leading into the vestibule. The sanctuary was traditional yet with its straight back, slip covered chairs it had the feel of a dining room. I tried to visualize the wedding that didn't happen as I sat in the sanctuary. If my parents had married there, the space would have accommodated the train on my mother's gown. It could have also allowed for the formality of my father in a morning coat and a striped cravat.

**

Havana was more beautiful than I imagined. Rather than decaying like the house in which I grew up, the city was in gorgeous ruins. Cuba was an aging beauty queen that rose above neglect and poverty. The place was translucent with pastel colors and light. Even Calle Mercéd 20 was painted in a light green. Mostly what I noticed was the people's hunger for all things American. Walking the streets of Havana was exhausting. Kids came up to me and asked me for *caramelitos* and *plumas*—candies and pens. I gave them one from a Boston nail salon that wrote in a frilly purple ink. Women who worked in a state-run pharmacy flagged me down on the street and asked if I had any medicine in my purse.

The black market in Havana has always been darker than *Noche Buena*—the Christmas Eve sky. Over the years people have traded anything from sex to money sent by relatives in America for a pound of meat or a cup of oil. My mother understood this system before its time. She had bartered with her father to come to the United States. She bartered with my father on just how much she was willing to lose herself in snowy, gray Connecticut. She had even bartered with the Portuguese cleaning women who rode the Asylum Avenue bus. Spanish and Ladino were close enough to Portuguese that my mother learned the language from a book called "501 Portuguese Verbs" to translate for them as she placed them in homes throughout West Hartford. In return, these women took turns rotating through our house to clean for half a day.

**

Daily charters to Cuba leave from the same terminal at Miami International Airport and the check-in is a veritable marketplace. Cuban ex-pats have emptied Costco, Target and Best Buy of televisions, microwaves, bicycles and air conditioners for their relatives still trapped in Cuba. Maybe that's how the people who live on Calle Mercéd 20 got their television. God Bless American materialism.

"God Bless America," my cab driver said in fractured English. He took me to the University of Havana. My mother claimed it as her alma mater, but she tells stories. I won't call them lies. Let's say they're wishful thinking. To his credit, Dad left my mother dancing with her fantasies. He never contradicted her when she said she was the Duchess of Albuquerque or she graduated from the University of Havana School of Social Work. The University of Havana didn't grant social work degrees. I knew this because one day, as I was interviewing my mother about her college years, I Googled at the same time. The dates didn't match her account. The university was closed down in November of 1956. But my mother swore she heard gunshots on her way to class when José Antonio Echevarria, the president of the University Students Federation, bled to death on the university's famous staircase. But Echevarria died storming Fulgencio Batista's presidential palace on March 13, 1957. That's five months unaccounted for in my mother's life.

I know my mother didn't want to think about the inconsistencies in her story. She just wanted it to be a good yarn starring her. But I saw the small café with a big banner behind the bar that announced the Federación Estudantil Universitaria—The University Students Federation. I asked my cab driver if Castro really plotted the revolution in that bar, but as we pulled away, he said was *aburrido* of history, of life in Cuba. The only thing he cared about was that his 30-year old Russian Lada taxi would start each morning and that he'd catch enough fares to put food on the table for his kids.

I know that *aburrido* means so much more than just boredom. It's a kind of lassitude mixed with the same Cuban melancholia I heard when my mother said how much she missed Cuba.

The driver had a mother-in-law in Jersey City who sent money whenever she could. It helped more than I could imagine, he said. When I went to pay him he asked me if I had any medicine—aspirin, antacid, anything—that I could spare. I gave him a half-bottle full of Advil and a 30 percent tip. He dropped me off at the Hotel Naciónal. Did Dad stay there when he went to Cuba for contract work as an accountant? A vacation to punch up his Spanish? Maybe my mother passed him on the street once upon a time. The crypto-American with the deep Central American tan.

Maybe I've dreamed this entire story. My mother always accused me of "inventing" things. But we Cubans have always told good tales, haven't we? We Cubans have always been wistful for the stories that no one talks about outside of our small bubble; for dreams that we shelter in our hearts and minds. Isn't that why my mother pulled down the shades and hid away to dance to Beny Moré on Saturday afternoons? To live out a life she inevitably had to keep secret?

En Havana llene'el campo. Todos lo quieren bailar. We are crypto-Latinos, dancing wildly because no one has found us out yet. And just like us, everyone in Havana yearns to dance.

Renée Ashley is the author of five volumes of poetry: *BECAUSE I AM SHORE I WANT TO BE SEA*; *BASIC HEART*; *THE REVISIONIST'S DREAM*; *THE VARIOUS REASONS OF LIGHT*; and *SALT*, as well as a novel, *SOMEPLACE LIKE THIS*, and two chapbooks, *THE MUSEUM OF LOST WINGS* and *THE VERBS OF DESIRING*. Ashley teaches poetry in the low-residency MFA Program in Creative Writing at Fairleigh Dickinson University. A portion of her poem, "First Book of the Moon," is included in a permanent installation in Penn Station, Manhattan, by the artist Larry Kirkland. Her new collection, *The View from the Body*, will be published by Black Lawrence Press in 2016.

From an Outdoor Table off the Carpark of an Uffculme Inn Waiting for Enterprise to Send Double-A to Assess the Problem with her Little Rented Car

Nothing is called what it is in that country It's been a strange few days Even Stonehenge she heard is not a real henge & the Slaughter Stone's never seen a body's-full of blood—its red stain an interface of iron & rain & soon she'll drive south—Cornwall Where she'll learn the touted palms aren't really palms at all but a different sort of monocot *Cordyline australis* known commonly as *cabbage tree* & oddly related to wheat A temperate species of tree—the Gulf Stream warms that Cornish coast—& it's food for the New Zealand Pigeon which actually lives in New Zealand but is frequently called *wood pigeon* though entirely different from the *Wood Pigeon (Columba palumbus)* which is also called *Ring Dove* & really if there's a god in heaven up there past those double-dealing birds why must this be so hard? An assembly of almost A stew of so-awfully-wrong At least a *Starling*'s still a *Starling* though *European* yet ensconced in the States Wretched nomenclature Cheeky bird & the pub she's at is closed 'til noon It's late December She'd packed again & locked the key inside her room Then the dash lights flashed the warnings she can't comprehend She thanks god for the cell phone she almost didn't bring for the new slick coat that presses her own warmth back on her But her fingers—which are writing this—are bare & ache as though since coffee they've been broken twice The clouds are breaking up The sky is bluing But a blue like that just lets more cold come down The inn is closed for one more hour Her help's not due for two & petrol's too dear to run the car to nowhere so she knows she'll sit it out outside This is the way she spells *vacation*—an indulgence she hasn't known since she drowned five hundred miles from home & awakened shamed & shuddering She was eight She's got one week to recall what fun's like Then back to the work desk But Uffculme's in Devon & the thing about Devon is a poet who lives there—a woman—she doesn't know where—who's written a poem on a river that shakes her to gasping every time It must be coruscating It's surely glimmering Perhaps there's something in the air she can learn from She hopes that's true She looks around Then here comes the chambermaid early for work Her rosiness seems permanent Fresh as fresh milk & wholesome Which reminds the one who's cold that she is not & yes the maid is entering but *Sorry* She's heading for the basement where the wash machines are kept *Oh no it's not the till of course but everything* She can't invite her in—on account of it's her job She needs it She's just the maid & so the thick door clicks behind the one & just before the other who shifts & shifts again Does everyone feel such tremors of faith? See simplicity crazing like glass? When she was younger When she thought she understood she was mistaken

Just last month in Rio the middle finger of the right hand of Christ appeared—after a terrible storm—to have broken a nail & now she's learned ligntning's lopped off his thumb Poor unopposable Christ No doubt it's his biscuit-dipping hand Even God's only soapstone & concrete son comes undone The stones of the world must be uniting They're standing up & falling down Corner stones & heel stones Keystones & whetstones Steppingstones plashing in waters where they don't belong & as though they're warm pebbles to hold in her hands she calls up the words she's recently heard *Trilithon* Three risen stones *Cursus* One long barrow *Sarsen* called *bluestone* called *sandstone* Called *Druid Stone* & *Greyweather* though Druids were too far-off & far too late Laggers in fact & the sun in its circuit in solstice in apogee & she in her flummox & bother & spit & recalling her friend who's dead but who when alive threw pots & glazed them in waves of a dull gray-green breaking on a dun–colored shore That friend said over & over again—waves making way on the shore of her ear—in a tone too sad to be feigned *If you want fair* she said again & again *you'll go to another booth* And it's true She knows it The words keep breaking over her *Ellipsis & occlusion Conceal & obstruct Omission Abandon Eclipse & Obscure* & still she has the moon for howling if she needs it but then again the new moon being no moon at all—a knowing that endlessly slays her—she'll have to plan ahead Yet someone will tell her her future She will hear it & misunderstand There's debris beneath the surface of the river that can snag a vessel Hold it down She believes things That's her problem Things rise & they fall & we're too often wrong The world we name is rich & we are approximate Even scientists were surprised the ribbed & endangered Mediterranean limpet (*Patella ferruginea*) can alter its gender to keep the species alive They know from a needle to the gonad Would that we were so flexible Nothing left really but to sit back & look To write it down Wait to be wrong Not such a bad life not such a crime

Before returning to his home state of Pennsylvania, where he teaches at Shippensburg University, **Neil Connelly** directed the MFA program at McNeese State. He has published five novels. His six, *Higher Ground*, is forthcoming from Arthur A. Levine.

People Like That, People Like Them

Because of a traffic jam caused by a nasty accident involving a jackknifed tractor-trailer, the Franklin family returned to Camp Hill late that Monday night, bleary-eyed and road weary from the turnpike. Over the long August weekend they'd spent at Andrea's in-laws in Pittsburgh, a trip on which Cassie had refused to eat anything but pancakes and Ellie had relapsed in her potty training, something in the guts of the upstairs toilet back home had sprung a leak. So when Andrea flipped on the kitchen light, it shone down on a good-sized puddle pooling on the linoleum. Immediately, she yelled for Mike, who was diligently unloading the minivan. Both the girls ran with him to the kitchen, and they found Andrea with her hands on her hips, staring up at the sagging ceiling. It looked bloated, ready to burst.

"Perfect," Mike said, stepping gingerly into the kitchen to better inspect the damage.

Ellie, always fearless, bolted out onto the slick floor and promptly slipped, whacking her head with a reverberating whomp. For a moment, it seemed to Andrea like the ceiling above her daughter might collapse.

The next morning, while the girls were watching cartoons and eating fruit bars on the couch, Mike called from the bank and told Andrea he'd contacted Krupka Brothers, a firm he'd helped with several loans. Tony Krupka would be sending over somebody before lunch, and they'd get started right away. Andrea, on her second cup of half-decaf, recognized this was great news, but she felt a faint but familiar tightness in her stomach. Before her husband hung up, he said, "Tony and his guys, they're good people."

"No doubt," she said. "I'll get ready for them. Thanks for taking care of this."

When the battered pickup truck pulled into her driveway two hours later, Andrea watched the thick man in the red t-shirt emerge from the driver's side. Middle-aged with a deep tan and huge boots, he was exactly what she anticipated in a handy man. She was surprised however by the second worker. She would place him in his late teens, and he was scrawny and chestnut-skinned, like the boys she saw on the TV in all those protests in the Middle East, the ones where one side had tear gas and the other had rocks, where flags were always burning.

In her youth, Andrea was shy, even mousy. She wouldn't qualify her feelings about strangers as an anxiety, but others had. As she pulled back the front door, she forced a smile, and the older man touched the brim of his baseball cap. "Mrs. Franklin? Got yourself a bit of a problem I hear."

"Yes," she said, and she stepped back to let them in.

The driver strolled inside, pausing to wipe his boots on the welcome mat. The dark-skinned boy followed. The girls, still in their flowing pajamas, came cascading down the stairs. "Who are they?" Cassie shouted, pointing a finger from the first step.

"Cassandra Lee!" Andrea said.

But the driver just grinned at the bad manners. He knelt and said, "I'm Mr. Jim. And this here is my helper, Steve."

Steve, who didn't make eye contact with anyone, dipped his head and shoulders in a sort of half bow acknowledgement, and Andrea wondered what his real name was. In an instant, she conjured a rich history for this teen, who'd surely fled ethnic conflict, been adopted perhaps, and now endured the stares of ugly Americans here in Central Pennsylvania. But when Steve said to the girls, "You two look like princesses," she was surprised to hear no trace of an accent.

Six steps up the staircase Ellie pulled out her pacifier, beamed a toothy smile, and said, "Pin-cess."

Jim nodded politely and rubbed his hands together. "So where's the patient?"

The two workers began by addressing first the simple origin of the problem, nothing more than a fractured connector valve in the toilet, then began removing the saturated ceiling. In great armloads, Steve carried the soggy chunks out to the bed of the pickup truck, heavy work that Andrea noticed Jim avoided. She spent the morning going about the standard chores that followed a trip, running the dust buster in the van, getting the laundry going, basic clean up. At one point, she remembered the turnpike accident and retrieved the laptop. She learned that the driver of the truck and four others, including an infant, were killed. When Mike slow rolled passed the scene, there was a minivan like theirs on its side in a ditch, the front end smashed in. Andrea had turned away, then checked to see if the girls were belted in properly. Skimming the article, she saw that police suspected a central factor in the accident was road rage.

This unsettled Andrea, even as she worked on a dinosaur puzzle with Ellie and made a Play Doh zoo with Cassie. On the living room floor, she played a game of Candy Land with both girls, carefully winding her way through the ominous Peppermint Forest and past the treacherous Gumdrop Falls.

She wanted to go out to run a couple errands, but she had mixed feelings about leaving the house unguarded. Sylvia from her book club had told her about workers "casing" a home for valuables, or pulling obscene pranks in the absence of owners.

In addition to the occasional chatter of the two men talking, Andrea heard another sound from the kitchen, what seemed to be a third voice. Jim and Steve had hung canvas tarps at both doorways to the kitchen, so she couldn't see what they were doing, and she couldn't be certain about this other person.

Around 1:00, just after Ellie complained of being "hun-gee," Andrea knocked on the doorframe and said, "Pardon me?" Almost immediately, as if he'd been waiting for her, Jim pulled back the tarp. He smiled warmly.

"Can I sneak in there, get to the fridge? I need to feed my daughters."

Jim glanced behind him, as if confirming a fridge was in fact in the room. "Sure, sure," he said. "Mind your footing."

Jim opened the tarp like a huge curtain and she crossed the threshold. Clear plastic was draped over the countertops and another thick tarp covered the floor. Every surface seemed dusted with powdery debris. When the job was finished, she'd need to scrub down the whole room.

Steve was at the peak of a V-shaped ladder next to the fridge, picking away at the edges of the gaping hole left by their demolition. She smiled at him, but her eyes shifted quickly to the underbelly of the second floor. Beams crisscrossed the opening, and pipes zigzagged along like a highway system. She could see part of the underbelly of the tub, and it was easy to figure out what corner the toilet was in. Unexpectedly, Andrea wasn't rattled by this. Rather, she liked seeing the sturdy inner workings of her home.

"Ain't nearly so bad as it could be," Jim told her. "It was a slow leak that mostly dripped straight down. Didn't do no real damage up above."

"Good," Andrea said, because she felt Jim wanted a response.

"I seen worse for sure. We got in before any mold took hold, and don't get me started on what Formosa termites'll do with wet wood."

Jim kept talking, but Andrea's focus shifted to the source of the third voice she'd heard earlier. It was her under-the-countertop radio, the one she used to listen to NPR sometimes when she was making dinner. Jim had clearly felt the right to not only turn on the radio, but to change the station. Coming through the speaker was the ranting and angry voice of an a.m. talk radio personality, one Andrea reviled for his mean-spiritedness and bigotry. He was talking now about a new immigration policy in Arizona and a union protest against Walmart outside Tucson that had erupted into violence. He said, "Only an idiot wouldn't see that these things are all connected."

Jim said, "We're just about done what we can do today. It needs to air out, dry some, and we'll be back tomorrow to patch up."

Andrea opened the fridge and pulled out two cartons of fruit yogurt. "Fine," she said. As she turned and passed Steve's ladder, something light glanced off her shoulder and fell onto the floor. Startled, Andrea dropped one of the yogurts, which exploded on impact.

"Hey jackhole!" Jim yelled. "Watch the lady!"

Andrea turned up to see Steve, staring down at her apologetically. He said, "I didn't know you was there."

"You alright?" Jim asked her.

She wiped her shoulder. "I'm fine," she told him. "Just caught me by surprise."

Jim glared up at Steve. "How many times I freakin' tell you—"

Andrea thought, *There's no need for that,* but said nothing. This rehearsal of dialogue was a longstanding habit. Instead of speaking, she retrieved another yogurt.

Jim grabbed a rag and began wiping up the mess. From his knees, shaking his head, he said to her, "Kids like this. You can't teach them a damn thing."

Kids like this, Andrea thought. She paused at the doorframe and looked back at Steve in the corner, expecting perhaps to share an awkward moment. But the boy had already gone back to work, hacking away at the ceiling above him with a saw-toothed knife.

That night, when Mike was inspecting the ceiling with some satisfaction, Andrea told him about the encounter.

"So what?" he said. "You've decided our drywaller is a racist?"

Mike had a habit of minimizing, even ignoring his wife's concerns, something that often made her wonder if they were valid in the first place. But here, she stood her ground. "I didn't call him that," she said. "It's just, I have a bad feeling about that guy."

Now Mike turned to her and cupped her shoulders. "Most of the work is done now. Tomorrow they'll hang the new ceiling, probably need to come back Wednesday for touch up. I'll paint it over the weekend and this little adventure will be in the books."

Andrea did take some comfort in the certainty in Mike's voice. They'd decided to eat out instead of dealing with the kitchen, and together they gathered their daughters for a trip to McDonald's.

Jim and Steve arrived the next morning just as Mike was leaving. From the bay window in the front of the house, Andrea watched the two older men talking animatedly, like they were old high school chums. Next to them, Steve hefted a large white bucket that looked heavy. He seemed uncertain if he should set it down. Andrea held her coffee mug with two hands, warming her palms. Behind her on the TV, Dora the Explorer shouted something in Spanish, and Ellie repeated, "ga-to!"

After greeting the workers she left them alone, again tending to her daughters and some household chores. Following a rousing game of Chutes and Ladders, Andrea decided a second morning show didn't make her a terrible mother, and she sat the girls down in front of *Word Girl* on PBS. *It's educational,* she thought. *It doesn't even count as TV.*

In the small study/guest room, she hopped online and paid a few bills, checked her email and Facebook account. There were photos posted by her sister-in-law from the weekend trip. Andrea didn't think she looked good, but she wrote "Great pictures!" in the comment.

One of her college friends had posted an article about a gay high school boy in Montana who'd been taunted to the point that he killed himself, right in the school cafeteria. No one knew how he'd snuck the rifle past the metal detectors. Therapists and sensitivity trainers were being called in. Andrea saw that the story had over a thousand "likes".

By the time she emerged from the study, Cassie was staring blankly at *Martha Speaks*, a show about a talking dog with an impressive vocabulary. The space where Ellie had been curled on the couch was empty. "Where's your sister?" Andrea asked. Cassie shrugged.

Unwilling to broadcast her negligence as a mother, Andrea didn't want to yell her daughter's name with the workers in the house, so she quickly went upstairs to the unmade beds and crayoned walls, then down to the basement, with castle parts strewn all over the floor. Before they left on the trip, she and the girls had spent hours setting up the castle's four impressive spires surrounding the central tower. Fleetingly, Andrea wondered when it had been destroyed.

Finally, with her heart racing just a bit, Andrea approached the heavy grey tarp that covered the doorway to the kitchen. She stretched out a hand, then when she heard Ellie giggle, she held it frozen in the air. Leaning in, she listened.

Jim said, "The important thing when you're painting is nice steady strokes, up and down. Just let that brush do the work."

Andrea tugged back the tarp and stuck her face through the opening, and she saw Ellie standing in front of the fridge, stroking it with a paint brush. Jim was on a short ladder, applying a white compound to the ceiling with a silver bladed tool. Eyes on the ceiling, he said, "Slow and easy. If you rush the job, you'll have to come back later. So slow and easy. Way better off doing it right the first time. Ain't that right, Steve?"

On another ladder, Steve was sticking thick white tape over what she saw as a fault line where a new piece of drywall met an old one. Andrea recalled a *60 Minutes* story about the boom in fracking for natural gas in Pennsylvania. Several studies suggested that out west, the industry's growth had led to an increase in seismic activity. On expert from Berkeley predicted a major earthquake.

Jim said to Ellie, "Don't let your brush go dry. Get you some more magic paint."

Ellie dipped her brush into a Tupperware container filled with water. "Ma-gic."

"Sweet girl," Jim said, trailing his eyes to Andrea.

She returned Jim's smile. "I'm so sorry she wandered in here. Kids can be a handful."

"Don't I know it," Jim said. "Got four myself. Two and two. We'll be finished up here right about lunch, then back tomorrow to sand this mud and put on a finishing coat. We hit a road bump or two. Genius-boy over there screwed up his cut line. But all in all the job's coming along just great. Just great."

"It looks so good," Andrea told them. "Thank you. Thank you both." She put extra emphasis on this, focusing on Steve, who hadn't paused in his work with the tape. Andrea admired how he'd ignored Jim's insult.

"Hey Skippy!" Jim snapped, and Steve turned. "The lady's talking to you."

Steve looked tired, tuned out. Andrea said, "I was only saying your work looked good. Come on Ellie, let's let the gentlemen finish." She held out a hand and her daughter followed her.

With lunch coming up, Andrea didn't want to interrupt the workers again, but she also didn't want to leave the house to bring the girls out. Sitting with the two of them at the dining room table, a whole buffet of Play Doh food spread out before them, Andrea thought of another idea. She reached for the laptop.

Just under thirty minutes later, the delivery boy knocked on the door. Andrea carried the steaming boxes to the dining room and went to the kitchen, where Jim and Steve were cleaning up. "I bought some pizza," she said. "Would you care to join us?"

"Ma'am?" Jim asked.

"In the dining room," Andrea explained. "For lunch."

Jim still looked perplexed.

"Free pizza," Steve said, wide-eyed.

But Jim hesitated. "That's very kind. Way we're all covered up though, we'd only make your nice dining room all dirty. No point in that. No point at all."

"Fine then," Andrea told him. "The table on the deck. We'll tell the girls it's a picnic."

The men stared at each other, and Andrea smiled. "I insist."

The impromptu meal was a great success. Jim told the girls a series of knock knock jokes while Steve devoured slice after slice. Andrea, who served iced tea from a pitcher, asked Steve where he grew up and he said, "Lemoyne," a town not five minutes away. Despite the absence of an accent, she'd still been hoping to hear something exotic, Cairo or Dubai.

At one point Cassie asked Jim what was on his arm, and he rolled back his short sleeve to reveal a circle of thirteen stars. "Those are for the original colonies. Are they teaching you about America at school?"

Cassie shook her head.

Jim curled his lips. "They ought to be. She's the greatest nation there ever was, God bless her."

Andrea wiped some pizza goop from Ellie's chin. "Cassie's only just heading in to third grade this year. They haven't done much history yet."

Jim set down his slice and sat back. "Nothing's more important. We're forgetting who we are in this country, I can tell you that."

"Who are we?" Cassie asked, and everyone laughed.

After they finished the pizza, Andrea got the girls ice pops, and she was delighted when Steve took an orange one. The men gathered their things and drove off, and Andrea left the girls in the backyard to play on the jungle gym. She went into the kitchen and inspected the work, which looked nice as far as she could tell. The ceiling had been made whole. Along the edges of the patch job was a thick white compound. Suddenly Ellie, sun-baked and thirsty, appeared at her side. Andrea retrieved a juice box and asked, "It looks good, doesn't it?"

Her daughter sipped on the straw.

"Those men, they were nice guys, huh?"

Ellie nodded and stopped drinking. She pointed to the ceiling, the corner by the fridge where Steve had been working. "Rag-head," she said.

Andrea caught her breath. "What?"

Ellie, beaming, repeated the word.

Andrea wasn't ten seconds into the phone call with Mike when he said "Calm down now," which she always found belittling. "Are you sure that's what she said?"

"No Mike. I'm calling you at work just to annoy you, just cause I've got nothing better to do." She hung up the phone.

That night, after leftover pizza, Mike bathed the girls, read them bedtime stories, and tucked them in. By the time he found Andrea on the couch, a short glass of red wine sat on the coffee table before her. She aimed the remote control at the TV, changed the channel. "I'm sorry," he said. "About when you called."

She kept her eyes on the screen.

"So let's say this guy did say that and Ellie overheard it. What do you want me to do?"

Andrea took a sip of her wine. "I don't want that man back in our house."

"Hang on now," Mike said. "Krupka told me he was his best guy, pulled him off a new construction job in Mechanicsburg to help me out. Tomorrow he's only got to be here for a bit. Be in and out in a couple hours probably. Then he'll be gone."

"I never want to see him again. And I don't want him near our daughters."

Mike ran a hand through his hair. "Sometimes guys say things. They don't mean anything by it."

"Is that what guys do, Mike? That's part of the man code?"

Mike plopped down in the Lazy-Boy and stared at the TV. A female reporter said that NASA was monitoring a Chinese communications satellite that had lost power. It was expected to burn up in the atmosphere, but some worried that small debris could rain down across the southeastern United States. Mike said, "Look, I'll call in to work in the morning. There's some things I can shuffle around. Would it make it better if I were here? If you didn't have to talk to the guy again?"

Andrea drained the last of the wine. "I don't want him near the girls. I'll take them to the park when he shows up."

But in the morning, it was raining. So when the pickup truck pulled along the front curb, Andrea shepherded the girls into the garage and headed for the mall. As she backed down the driveway, she saw Jim and Steve crossing the lawn, crouched against the rain. Steve was carrying the toolbox.

As she wandered the Camp Hill mall with her daughters in tow, Andrea's eyes kept falling on those not like her. Browsing at the entryway to a bookstore, an Indian woman with a red dot above her nose; an Asian men working at a kiosk selling hot pretzels; at the indoor playground, two African-American mothers with children about the same age as Ellie and Cassie. The kids fell in together easily, talking and playing without regard for skin color. Andrea wondered if the mothers, who were both beautiful in the same way, could be sisters, but she didn't want to ask such a personal question.

An older man Andrea identified as Mexican came hobbling into the playground pushing a stroller with a sleeping child, likely his grandson. He parked the stroller and pulled out a cell phone. Andrea knew that every one of these people she saw at the mall, the people not like her, had surely dealt with men like Jim, narrow-minded men who judged in ignorance. Andrea saw the sisters whispering and when she glanced at the grandfather, he averted his eyes. She became overcome by the strange sensation that the sisters and the grandfather somehow knew what she had done, or rather hadn't done. They were all talking about her right now. Andrea decided they'd be right to be disappointed. She would no longer be bullied into silence in the face of hatred.

So even though the two hours wasn't up, Andrea summoned the girls and told them to put on their Crocs.

As she drove home, she mentally composed the email—or even better, the certified letter—that she would send to Tony Krupka. The phrases floated through her mind: "unacceptable in this day and age," "utterly repulsive behavior," "tainting the innocent soul of my daughter." She would demand action, insist that Jim be disciplined or fired or forced into diversity training.

When she turned the corner onto Beverly Drive, the pickup truck was still in front of her house, and Jim and her husband were standing by it, smiling the way men always did. The rain had passed through. Andrea didn't look their way as she pulled up the driveway into the open garage. She released the girls into the living room, telling them they could watch one show while she prepared lunch.

Steve was in the kitchen, alone, sweeping up the floor. The countertops were immaculate, the ceiling pristine. The teen didn't lift his head when she walked in on him. He bent and extended one hand with a dustpan.

"Thank you for cleaning up," Andrea said. "It looks great."

"Glad you like it, ma'am."

"You do good work."

"I'm learning."

Between them, there was a silence. Mike came in the front door, and the two of them heard him chatting with the girls. Steve finished sweeping, returned the broom to its closet, and moved toward the exit.

"Wait," Andrea said, lowering her voice. "I have to tell you something."

Steve stopped in the threshold and turned.

Andrea inhaled once, deeply, then let out the breath. "I'm sorry."

"Sorry for what?"

"For not sticking up for you yesterday. But I'm going to now. I'm going to do the right thing, like all of us should. I'm going to write a certified letter. People like you don't deserve people like him."

After a moment, Steve scratched the back of his neck. "I'm not sure what you mean. People like who?"

"Jim," she whispered. "He's horrible to you. And I know the kind of language he uses. That's hateful and cruel and is absolutely unacceptable in our day and age." She felt a lightness in her chest as she delivered this line.

Steve shrugged and said, "What now?"

Andrea pressed her palms together and it was decided. She spoke the word, saying it as if she was spitting out something foul.

Steve stared at her and she said, "That's what my daughter said. My sweet little girl called you that because that's what she heard Jim call you. He's teaching her hate, right in my home. I teach my children not to judge others."

Steve's face scrunched up, as if he were trying to work out a complex mathematical equation. Finally he said, "Ma'am, that dude's an asshole for sure and for certain. He runs me pretty hard, but I get paid under the table and I've learned a ton this summer. Yesterday he gave me serious shit cause his cutline was smooth and mine was all ragged. He had to cut mine again himself, even it out, and he was explaining it all to your kid, my screw up and everything. She was in here painting then. Jim was really rubbing it in, point at his line and mine and repeating *smooth* and *ragged* over and over."

Andrea could think of nothing to say, so she said, "Oh."

From out front, a truck horn blared. Steve stood there for a few seconds, then turned and walked away.

After he was gone, Mike joined Andrea in the kitchen. With his face tilted up, he said, "They do quality work." Andrea, who was wiping down the already cleaned countertops, didn't answer. Mike stepped up behind her and said her name. She stopped and turned around and her husband put a hand gently on either shoulder. "For what it's worth," he said. "I think you were right about that guy. He gave me the creeps. Out front just now, he kept ranting about our sacred duty to America as the land of the free. He even has a bumper sticker, one of those *America, love it or leave it!* deals." Mike grunted and shook his head. "People like that. I'll never understand them."

Andrea slid into her husband's chest and let his arms close around her. She knew she'd never tell him the truth.

As Mike embraced her, Andrea's eyes lifted to the ceiling, which was restored and flawless. Except for the slight shift in whites, it was impossible to tell where the patch work ended and where the original was. After Mike painted, it would be good as new, forgotten.

Monic Ductan has an M.F.A. in fiction from Georgia College. Her recent work has appeared or is forthcoming in *Shenandoah, Big Muddy, So to Speak,* and *Tahoma Literary Review.* She was a spring 2013 runner-up for the Diana Woods Memorial Award in nonfiction and a fiction finalist for the Agnes Scott College Writers' Festival Contest in spring 2015. Monic lives in Mississippi.

How to Be Massaged by a Man You Think You No Longer Love

Stretch out on your belly,
Arms in front like Superman,
So he can press his fingers
Under your scapulae. When he says,
I like the way you are put together,
Close your eyes and imagine
Him taking you apart.
When his fingers break the skin,
And nails scrape taut flesh,
Pray he doesn't touch the spine,
That part of you so brittle
It may leave you no choice but to say,
I love you. If the spine holds, you'll be
Damned if he squeezes a lung,
Makes you wheeze, *I love you,*
For mercy. If you are lucky—
If for dinner you've had a rabbit's
Foot wrapped in four leaf clovers—
He won't touch the heart.
Maybe the steam off its chambers,
Hot as an overworked machine,
Will cause him to draw away,
Oblivious to chambers trembling.

Translator's Note
This original poem appeared in the collection *From the Other Side* (1965) in the middle of Francisco "Paco" Urondo's writing career. Paco's poetry became increasingly committed and conversational from this moment forward in response to the growing repression of the Argentine state, though in "Loving Her Is Difficult" his revolutionary ideology and imagery is already prominent. In 1976, at the age of 46, due to his militant activism on and off of the page, Paco was publicly killed in Mendoza by the police. His work has largely remained untouched by critics and anthologies, so this translation is a work of advocacy for a poet of great talent, of humor and pain, with much to contribute to the international community of writing. I have translated for the original message, movement, and sound, but I also made choices for the pleasure of the English.

Francisco "Paco" Urondo (poet) was a prolific writer who published novels, short fiction, and plays, though primarily poetry; he famously produced an interview conducted in prison, "La patria fusilada," making known the testimonies of the three survivors of the Trelew massacre. Paco was a target of Argentine state violence, but had a rich writerly life, and was named Director of Culture in Santa Fe, Argentina, in 1958. Paco's assassins were finally convicted in 2011.

Julia Leverone (translator) is a PhD candidate in Comparative Literature at Washington University in St. Louis. She has her MFA from the University of Maryland. Her original poems and translations have appeared or are forthcoming in publications such as *Witness, Poetry International, Cimarron Review, Asymptote, Crab Orchard Review, B O D Y*, and *Tupelo Quarterly*. She is Editor of the D.C.-based *Sakura Review*. Her chapbook, *Shouldering*, is forthcoming from Finishing Line Press.

Loving Her Is Difficult

It's good when she sleeps:
the heat of her body is a dagger of glass
that pierces dreams.
When she quiets, it is good,
her voice a forgotten premonition, perilous,
wrecking silence.
When she shouts or cries
or worries or relishes or tires,
nothing can contain
the lively pain poisoning
my loneliness.
That's why it's difficult
to think of her, her kind face,
to give over;

is cowardice to keep her
and to let her go, a terrible cruelty.
Sometimes, considering it,
I don't know what to do with her,
with this destiny, its light.

Amarla es difícil
Es buena, cuando duerme;
el calor de su cuerpo es un puñal de vidrio
que remonta los sueños.

Cuando calla, es buena
y su voz una premonición olvidada y peligrosa
que arruina el silencio.

Cuando grita o llora
o se lamenta o se divierte o se cansa,
nada puede contener
este dolor alegre que envenena
mis sueños y mi soledad.
Por eso es difícil pensar
en ella, en su cara bondadosa;
abandonarse; por eso
es una cobardía retenerla
y dejarla ir, una pavorosa crueldad.
A veces, cuando lo pienso,
no sé qué hacer con ella,
con este destino luminoso.

J. P. Dancing Bear is editor for the *American Poetry Journal* and Dream Horse Press. Bear also hosts the weekly hour-long poetry show, Out of Our Minds, on public station, KKUP and available as podcasts. He is the author of thirteen collections of poetry, his latest book is *Love is a Burning Building* (FutureCycle Press, 2014). His work has appeared or will shortly in *American Literary Review*, the *2014 Poet's Market* and elsewhere.

Aubade

First song of the mourning doves and I awaken like the cursed
to find the happiness in a dream dismissed. *I should sleep more*
I tell myself—enjoy that otherness. Sometimes the ashes
in my eyes are only felt when light hits them. Then the burning,
as the sun were in the room, charring away fantasy.
I pull my clothes on and begin to move away from the bed
not looking back at my fading impression upon the mattress.
A single flake of ash feathers against my lip as I walk.

•

We move like trained dancers. Close, catching the other
at all the moments where one could spin off into a new orbit,
saved for the perfection of your hand in mine. Effortless movement
as we glide through our naked lengths, as though we are autumnal
trees coming to life with wind. This is the dream left every dawn:
where I have touched you and you've touched back.

Jed Myers lives in Seattle. Two of his poetry collections, *The Nameless* (Finishing Line Press) and *Watching the Perseids* (winner of the 2013 Sacramento Poetry Center Book Award), are 2014 publications. His work has received *Southern Indiana Review*'s Editors' Award, the *Literal Latte* Poetry Award, a Pushcart nomination, and, in the UK, a Forward Prize nomination. His poems have appeared in *Prairie Schooner, Nimrod, Crab Orchard Review, Fugue, Painted Bride Quarterly, Crab Creek Review, The Citron Review*, and elsewhere.

Movie Day

My cousin and I have been cruising all day
in his mother-in-law's old black Cadillac

on the streets of LA, but it could be
Moscow or London or Lincoln, Nebraska.

We would be caught on enough keen lenses
wherever we were—even out where

the hawks and ospreys watch for their vertebrate
prey in the rivers and brush. There are

enough receptors, counting the wet-ware
we creatures bear, along with the countless

cameras mounted on lampposts, in cabs
and elevators, behind the clerks

in the quick-shops, high in the corners
of pawnshops and banks...and of course

the capture through the lenses of so many
phones, let alone the wide-open

eyes of kids we imagine could not be
paying attention—enough vision

and ready memory, enough overlap
in all these fields of perception, close

enough to a sort of *Sensurroud* grasp
embracing the world with witness to call it

an incessant cinema, a consummate
biopic of our being manifest

now and now and now. We haven't

a chance to edit it, to edit

ourselves out of it—we are cast
as we are. At the moment my cousin

and I have arrived in Hollywood, under
whatever satellite registers two

unremarkable human figures about
to walk into Musso & Frank's for a bite

in the old class landmark. Our eyes take
a minute out of the blaze to adjust

to the dreamy interior light. We slide
smooth arcs over blood-toned leather and there

we are where our greeter's posed us, under
the ceiling's broad beams, in a scene

staged for us since 1919
when the silents were just moving west. Isn't this

place a chapel of cocktails and steaks?
And there's its altar, a hissing black

iron grill in its tower of bricks.
I picture the bovine ocular aperture

instants before the kill, ponder
the cool choreography of the slaughterhouse

crew somewhere back in the Midwest
I guess…. This production's immense—

just the backdrop for us to review
the rushes we've saved from takes in our kitchens,

living rooms, bedrooms, when who knew
we'd make anything of it! Decades

confused, and what can be spliced
together today? I'm thinking sliced

tomato and ripe avocado, before
anything else. He'll do the Caesar.

There was our shared great-grandfather, watching
America swell at the normal ten million

frames of neural impression per second
from where he stood on the deck. Whatever

his name was, it's captioned nowhere. Or is it
everywhere, however dispersed

in the atmosphere and the earth? And this
an absurdist documentary, if

you'll think of it that way. Let's call it
the *docu-surd*. No one is catching

anywhere near the whole thing—we're busy
being on set, and we hardly know it.

Even the sallow little old man
in his elegant red waistcoat writing

our wishes for the fried oysters down
on his notepad is a participant. I am

one of the camera dollies, trained
at present upon his thin silver hair,

and sound is on, through my ears, gathering
under-notes of his bitterness

beneath his officious Eastern European
accent. I'm zooming in,

aren't I? Why do I
go close-up on this? I'm just wondering

how the collecting device we call
his eye feeds into the part of the movie

he unwittingly directs. It fits
that I come to this dizzy discovery here

in LA, in Hollywood, where
we got seriously into making the footage

we'd play and harvest into our hearts
in the theaters. Now I see everyone's given

a part. It is pleasantly dark
in this yesteryear haunt where they serve you

too much, and it isn't
about the food, but it could be

the ghost of many an old star seated
in the next booth. This is like being

among those luminous characters who sang
and danced and leapt and orated and wept

our hopes, woes, and terrors away
one war to the next, till they were swept

off the lots, terminally gray and breathless
after too many cigarettes—this is

where some might've lunched and cinched
their parts in the day, in their hats

and suits and pearls, while we were born
and fed and grown and taken to watch

those immense women and men defend
our honor for us in the great dark houses.

We are served the grotesquely huge
oysters in their thick batter coats,

and our Manhattans have come, adorned
each with one *Technicolor*-red cherry.

My cousin and I have gotten to talking
about our fathers, how they were

lost in their well-learned rolls. It's as if
we see them dance across the white tablecloth

dressed as they were for work, ties
tight at their necks, pleated pants pressed,

acting as if they were being watched
by an audience, but not by us.

Patti Crouch's writing has appeared in various journals, including *Pilgrimage, Bellingham Review, Bayou Magazine* and *Literary Mama*. Though she grew up in the Rockies, she's lived and taught in Northwest logging towns, a Japanese fishing village and the Puget Sound suburbs. Currently she lives in Washington State with her husband and sons.

Cup of Grace

For his tenth Christmas, we bought him junior magic tricks—a silk scarf, bright nestling cups, an odd rimmed pouch, a wand filled with sand that hissed when you tipped it sideways. Our son practiced before his mirror, the instruction pamphlet opened on his dresser, muttering the script as his fingers fumbled with plastic. He loved Houdini, so I brought biographies from the library that we studied side by side: chained Houdini suspended like a fish, or poised to leap from a winter's bridge, or peering above the lip of a custom-made milk can. In one poster, his body dissolves into a swirl of green mist and seeps through a coffin's walls. In my favorite photo, young Houdini grins beside a famous magician while stretching his feet into elegant tiptoes. In every headshot, his gray eyes glare at the camera, mesmerizing.

In a self-portrait my son did that year, at the private school where I taught and where we sent him with dreams of glory, my son glares from black paper. His hair shines blonde against bands of angry red clouds, and his black shirt darkens all below. This was the winter he refused to cut his hair or hug, the winter his skinny body seemed wrapped in quiet misery, the winter he asked why we had to be so poor, why our house was so small, why no one called back. At recess he never played but ran laps around the playground, like a swallow circling low before a storm. In that spring of pounding rain and wind, giant firs toppled down hillsides as I lay sleepless. The bay shone a perpetual slate gray. The next year, on an autumn day sparkling with sunshine, I left our son at our local public school, leaned my forehead on the steering wheel and sobbed.

I suppose in his tenth year we still believed in magic, the idea that through intention and practice he could transcend the boundaries of human limitations and reveal his amazing power. What he got were black-and-white photos and a box of plastic trinkets.

I wonder still about magic and grace and about how we raise our children. In the Y locker room yesterday, a woman raved about her nails, painted in polish that changed color with temperature. She plunged her fingers into cold water and her friends gasped, "Look at that! It's changing!" I wonder about the spectacle of magic, the breathless "Ta da!" that leaves the audience asking, "How'd he do that?" I wonder how quickly the joy of such a moment subsides. And I wonder about grace. After our return from a trip this week, neighbors arrived with laughter and dahlias and an overflowing bowl of strawberries. My blueberry bushes were covered with berries big as my fingertips that I plucked as delicately as a possum's lips, one by one. To wrench snaps the tiny twig, so that unripened berries fall, wasted. I stood in the sunshine and twisted carefully, filling a bowl and marveling at the berries' warmth in my mouth, the smooth round skin and splash of sweetness. I think of grace as plumping from within, an invisible presence, a glowing warmth that pushes tough green potential into sustenance.

Years ago on a hillside above my parents' home, I had a hideout. The land there was harsh, with blazing heat in the summer and swirling snowstorms in the winter, a land desiccated and scarred with gullies and boulders toppled from ridgelines. Everything seemed prickly--dried grasses, rough composite stone, pine trees and clumps of cactus hiding beneath sagebrush. I stepped carefully, listening always for the buzz of rattlesnakes. But desolation brought freedom. On that steep hillside rested a massive boulder, broken like an egg, one half embedded into the earth and the other toppled forward diagonally. A soft hillock shielded one side of the egg's crevice, and on the other rose the silvery trunk of a giant ponderosa, its dried limbs twining upwards like frozen smoke. The wind and sun didn't penetrate this space, and even in the deepest snowstorms, the small hollow between the stones was soft, unruffled sand. If I traced my fingers through it, spiraling around a pebble or a mouse's dried jawbone, the lines remained until I swept them away. If I belly-crawled to the front boulder's edge, I could see over the next ridge to a cottonwood grove, incongruously lush, that held a tiny cottage. To the left, snaking between the mountain and Immigrant Gap, was the highway to town and beyond. When I returned to my hideout years ago with my husband and young sons, I was startled by wind whistling between the boulders and light that seemed wrong. The great ponderosa had fallen, its boughs splayed across the hillside and dissolving into earth.

Almost daily I wonder—how should we raise our children? As a teenager, my husband cooked Swanson dinners in a dreary succession while his mother did rounds at the hospital; I still say my best childhood friend was my old gray horse and the quiet hills above an overpacked house. But we belong now to a generation of parental busyness, of competition that simmers like a silently screaming teakettle. I've stood, smile frozen and brain calculating, as a mother enumerates her child's latest accomplishments in the midst of determined enrichment—Kumon math, chess club, soccer on a *select team*—wondering how much is enough or too much, or how far behind we fall. "Oh my God, we're so busy," I hear again and again, see parents in a half-run as they shuttle between activities, and I fear we've gotten it all wrong.

There's something terrifying about raising a child. From the time I held my first infant, I've whispered, "Please, God, let me die first." I think sometimes we cherish our progeny so deeply that all threats--from fatal accidents or drug abuse or suicide, to inadequate soccer time or a disappointing teacher—loom like fanged monsters, the lot of them so horrifying that there's no sorting the essential from the trivial, no questioning of what's irrational and what will pass with time and fortitude. I remember one summer, watching as the swallows, nested in our porch, swept back and forth to press insects into the gaping beaks of their insatiable young. As their feathers tufted out in raggedy fluffs above their skinny bodies, I feared they'd drop from the sky in sheer exhaustion. My best moments of parenting, the memories I hold in a bubble of tenderness, are the idle hours I spent with my sons on my lap, a stack of books before us, turning page after page because I couldn't think of anything else to do. I miss the sweet illustrations, the sometimes-clever wordplay, the warm soft body snuggled so close that the boundaries of skin nearly disappeared.

Last autumn our newspaper announced the Northern Lights would be visible from our latitude, and when the weekend forecast looked clear, we threw sleeping bags into our camper van and drove toward the coast. Everyone was grouchy—a Friday after school and work, our favorite campground already filled—but we found a last sliver of concrete between two massive RV's. Despite campfire, hot dogs and s'mores, nothing cut the bristly weariness. After dark, as we walked across a field shadowed by massive evergreens, my son slipped beside me, and I felt a warm hand seek mine. I held it, soft as a baby bird cradled in my fingers. When the trail turned and the lingering twilight of ocean and sky opened before us, his hand slipped away and I knew it was the last time. My fingers held air, an aureole like a saint's blue breath or the pulsing of fireflies. We never saw the Northern Lights, only clouds streaked red with the sunset's echo. But as we walked back to our van, from the darkness we heard laughter and crackling campfires and the incongruous snap of a Ping-Pong game. Perhaps that night as we slept, electricity danced in waves of yellow and green above us, a silent wavering of hosannas across the midnight sky.

I knew a woman once who'd been buried by an avalanche, curled in a womb of snow and ice through the night and half a morning, until the rescuers seeking a body found her alive. She told a reporter, "I've been given a new metaphor for grace." When I saw her later at a party--willowy and blonde, smile bright as a snowfield, her gestures quiet as fluttering leaves on summer evenings when a breeze sweeps away the day's heat—I wanted to touch her arm and reassure myself she was real. I don't know what you see when you pass onto the other side and nestle there, suspended in darkness and cold under a winter sky, don't know what touching death teaches you about life. But I imagine it's like plucking an apple from the ancient tree in our church's courtyard, the one that neighborhood children climb to drop fruit into their parent's hands, to carry home in overstretched t-shirts. On the walk home my son's shoulder brushes mine and we move in the silence of gratitude.

Lois Marie Harrod's 13th and 14th poetry collections, *Fragments from the Biography of Nemesis* (Cherry Grove Press) and the chapbook *How Marlene Mae Longs for Truth* (Dancing Girl Press) appeared in 2013. *The Only Is* won the 2012 Tennessee Chapbook Contest (Poems & Plays), and *Brief Term*, a collection of poems about teachers and teaching was published by Black Buzzard Press, 2011. *Cosmogony* won the 2010 Hazel Lipa Chapbook (Iowa State). She is widely published in literary journals and online ezines from *American Poetry Review* to *Zone 3*. She teaches Creative Writing at The College of New Jersey. Read her work on www.loismarieharrod.org.

Kite

What happens is predictable:
anything made by hand

objectifies, so we shouldn't say
it has a right to live.

The possessive parent fits the child
into his own flight, selfish

and self-satisfied. Who's surprised
when the string tangles

or floats away?

Martha Silano's books include *The Little Office of the Immaculate Conception* and *Reckless Lovely*, both from Saturnalia Books, and, with Kelli Russell Agodon, *The Daily Poet: Day-By-Day Prompts For Your Writing Practice* (TwoSylvias Press 2013). Her poems have appeared in *Paris Review, Poetry, American Poetry Review, North American Review* (where she received the 2014 James Hearst Poetry Prize), *Best American Poetry 2009*, and elsewhere. Martha edits *Crab Creek Review* and teaches at Bellevue College.

Doomed Moon

Saturn's rings may have been created by an unnamed moon that disappeared 4.5 billion years ago – The Daily Galaxy

An unnamed moon.
    Baby Bianca, Darling Dione.
Her outer layers wintry.
    On a morning stroll in her Britax B-Agile,
unwittingly whammed
    into something larger, something saturnine,
someone in need
    of her lucent cold,
her frost-bound frigorific.
    A big thing wants to be bigger;
Saturn signed on as accomplice.
    Not a moon-on-moon clash
or the rings would be rocky.
    Doomed moon diving
toward death,
    bereft of its bluster;
doomed moon unnamed,
    neither Janus nor Fornjot,
not Hyperion nor Pallene,
    gelid stripped away on impact,
hydrogen shroud
    inducing a knack for creating/
destroying. For a thousand decades
    the spiraling loops
ten to a hundred times larger.
    Icy spheres birthing
the new—Epimetheus, Tethys.
    Alterations, actions,
anything but static:
    all this doomsday drama,
all this shimmery ruination.

Marc Morgenstern is a lapsed journalist, TV news producer and music executive. His short stories have been published in *Soundings Review, Klipspringer* and *Digital Papercut*. Marc's non-fiction work has appeared in *The New York Times, The Huffington Post, The Christian Science Monitor* and the *Times* of Trenton NJ, where he once covered the mob-controlled garbage industry. He attended the 2014 Yale Writers' Program (Instructors: Rick Moody and Teddy Wayne) and is a serial participant in the UCLA Writers' Program (Instructor: Lou Mathews). Marc traveled across the U.S. with an original copy of the Declaration of Independence, an experience that he presented on The Moth's Los Angeles stage. From his home in Santa Monica, CA, he frequently cycles long distance to work out plot issues.

Cellophane Boy

When my mother found out that she had a killing disease, she decided to teach me everything she could before she died. So, over her last three months, I sat on the end of her bed and learned things like how many tines were in a dinner fork (four), how to take a compliment (just say thank you), how to always flatter a girl's choice of shoes (those shoes make your legs look so long), and how, when I was old enough to wear long pants and a hat, I should always take off my hat when I go inside. Respect and courtesy, she said.

She died in 1944, having taught me everything except what I most wanted to know — how to live when your mother was gone.

During the funeral service, I sat next to my father in the first row. He wore his grey fedora, which was allowed for grown-up men. I put my hand on top of his hand, all freckled and damp, and he let it stay there. Normally, he wasn't a touchy kind of Dad, so that was something.

"I know how you felt about her," he said. That was a lot of words for my father. He didn't talk much and when he did, his words usually came out in one flat tone, like they had been washed too many times. There were never any of the nice colors that came from my mother's mouth. She had talked enough for both of them.

My father was called up to chant the Kaddish. I wasn't even thirteen yet, so I stayed alone in the pew. Barely lit by a single brass floor lamp, the coffin seemed to be disappearing, as if it was already half buried. Didn't they know my mother was scared of the dark?

That night after the Shiva, my father and I shared a stew that Mrs. Schwartz had brought over from next door. He ladled out carrots and celery and meat from the pot onto my plate, and then his, and sat down next to me.

"There's something we need to talk about," he said.

That was alarming to me because the last time he used those words, my mother had just taken sick. I studied my plate with its web of cracks, like veins, and a crust of overcooked noodles left from dinner the night before. My mother would have made sure the plate was properly washed. My father cleared his throat. He told me he was moving in with a woman who had a new baby.

I wanted to run, but my legs didn't seem to work anymore. Inside my skull was an ocean of noise that included my mother's voice, saying "Shush, Joshee, it's going to be all right." No, it's *not* going to be all right. Rather than saying anything to my father, I decided at that moment to be as quiet as he had always been, quieter even. I would become invisible, a cellophane boy.

The next day, he delivered me and my wicker suitcase to his sister Rose's. We climbed the steep stairway to my aunt's second floor dress shop with the small apartment behind it.

"It's better this way," he said from several steps below me. "You don't want all that fuss of having a baby around."

I pushed through the door at the top of the stairs into a bright hall of mirrors. Women liked to see what the back of their dress looked like as much as the front, so Rose had installed walls of facing mirrors. I could see my reflection echo and shrink into almost nothing: a short boy in short pants with a nose that didn't quite fit his face yet. Then, my father in his fedora appeared, breathing heavily and multiplied in the mirrors.

"Rose!" He put down the suitcase and removed his hat. He was bald underneath — that kind of baldness where the naked spot perches in the middle surrounded by a furry halo of hair.

"Coming, Mort." She was midway into removing her kitchen apron, revealing a flowered dress with a very large chest. You could see she had just applied fresh rouge for her older brother.

"Oh, Joshua." She buried me in a hug. Then we all looked at each other without speaking for a long time; no one seemed to know what to do next. Finally, my father picked up the suitcase and went into the kitchen.

He was already sitting at the small pine table when we came in, his hat stationed in front of him. I could see the worn, matching dimples on the crown where his thumb and second finger raised and lowered it. My grandmother, wrinkled and toothless, sat beside him sipping tea through a wooden straw. A small cot with an olive army surplus blanket had been set up in the corner.

"I expect that you will have certain reimbursable expenses for the boy," he said to Rose.

"Re-im-burs-able?" she said, syllable by syllable, as if the word was in some foreign language.

"You know, food and clothes and such. And I've thrown in a little extra for your trouble."

My Grandma loudly slurped her tea, brewed with a reused tea bag. Though she only spoke in Yiddish, she understood English well enough to know what her son had said: that her grandson was trouble and you had to pay somebody to take care of that. She slurped louder this time, but didn't say a word. Hiding in the shadow cast by the lone window, I stayed quiet, too.

My father reached into the inside pocket of his suit coat and pulled out a folded wad of green bills. I had seen men with silver money-clips that flashed when lifted from their dark pockets into the light. But my father's money-clip was a red rubber band.

He licked the tip of his first finger and counted out seven one-dollar bills onto the table. Everyone stared at the small pile for a few seconds until my father rose and carefully re-positioned his hat.

"Next Friday, then," he said, and walked out.

When he reappeared each Friday, Aunt Rose would offer him tea and Ritz crackers straight from the box. I would try to stay invisible in the shadow by the window, but he always asked how school was going. I said "Fine." The kitchen smelled of peppermint tea, Pine-sol and the flowery perfume that Rose favored. He would count out seven bills and leave.

His Friday visits always took place between the four and seven o'clock shows at the Loew's Theater up on the Grand Concourse, where he was the manager. It was a grand hall, full of gold leaf and velvet seats, so being the manager there was an important job. Rose said he was very good at business and very strict with how he ran the place.

One Saturday, I snuck in the exit door after the newsreel had started. I let the heavy door slam, hoping to be caught by a red-uniformed usher and sent to the manager's office for a scolding. People loudly shushed me from the dark, but I never was nabbed. In the lobby afterwards, I hunted for him in the flow of chattering people arriving for the next show. I suppose I could have asked him for a free ticket anytime. Somehow, I was always afraid that if I asked, he would say "no." Company policy, or something like that.

One Thursday, Aunt Rose asked me to hand-deliver a pale blue dress box to an unfamiliar address a few blocks away. I welcomed these trips so I could escape the kitchen where I ate, studied and slept.

I ran to a fancy stone building, guarded by a doorman with gold braids on his shoulders. His white-gloved hand waved me to an elevator. I rang the doorbell and tried my best to deepen my voice. "Delivery!" I announced. "Delivery from Rose's Dress Shop!" I wanted to impress this woman. In my experience, the more efficient I sounded, the better the tip I received.

The red-haired woman who opened the door was younger than my mother, but older than a high school girl. She would have been pretty except that she obviously needed sleep and hadn't bothered to cover her mask of tiredness with face powder or anything. She balanced a baby in the crook of one arm like a football and held a baby bottle in her free hand.

"So you must be Joshua." It was a weary statement of fact, just a name.

"Yes, ma'am. Sent by my Aunt Rose with a package." I grinned like someone worthy of a tip.

"Ah, Rose. Best dressmaker in the Bronx," she said, forcing a little smile.

"Thanks, ma'am." I could see a corner of the room beyond the door. There was an expensive-looking gold couch with cushions so thick they seemed pumped up with air. The red and gold rug was woven like a maze and looked deep enough to swallow my toes.

The baby began to fuss so the woman placed the bottle in its little mouth.

Her smile disappeared. "A dress. He's going to have to do more than that," she said to no one in particular.

I didn't know what she was talking about and wanted to get going. "Package?" I reminded her.

"Oh, right. Just put it on the table." She tilted her head towards a glossy black table just inside the door. On it sat an old-fashioned candlestick telephone and a grey fedora with two scarred dimples. I set the blue box down.

"Daphne, who is it?" It was my father's voice coming from another room. Now, I knew for absolute sure that she was the woman who had replaced my mother one day after the funeral, and this was their baby, and it didn't look very new. By the time she answered, "Your son," I was on my way out the door.

The next night at Rose's apartment, my father kept his hat on. That particular Friday, the fifth since my mother's death, he didn't even sit down. He planted his hands on the kitchen table and leaned in like he was about to give a speech. He wasn't a tall man, but he seemed tall to me in that grey suit with the heavily padded shoulders.

There were no crackers or tea. Rose, Grandma and me sat at the little table, looking up at him, waiting a long time for him to say something. Aunt Rose had a new look on her face, a tight clench of bad expectations – fear, even.

He pulled the thick wad of money from his suit coat. He lifted it to his eyes and turned it over and over again, examining it close and long enough to commit the government numbers on the bills to memory, if he had wanted to. Then, he very quickly buried it back in his pocket.

He stared down at the pine table as if an answer was carved there. "You're old enough," my father said. And then he looked right at me. "You'll be fine."

He stood and tilted his hat forward in preparation for leaving the darkening apartment -- a bald, grey man in a grey hat with a woman and a baby. He grabbed the glass doorknob and stopped. I thought he had something more to say -- something important. Instead, he reached in the left pocket of his suit coat. He flipped a small shiny disk towards me.

I could have caught it easily. I could see it was a quarter -- a decent amount of change in 1944 for a kid. I let it sit there on the floor, a piercing circle of light, as night visited and the door slammed.

Sharon Hashimoto teaches at Highline College in Des Moines, Washington. Her book of poetry, *The Crane Wife*, was co-winner of the Nicholas Roerich Prize and published by Story Line Press in 2003. She is a recipient of a National Endowment for the Arts fellowship in poetry. Her stories and poetry have appeared in *North American Review*, *Crab Orchard Review*, *Bamboo Ridge*, *Tampa Review*, *Shenandoah*, and many other literary publications.

On Hearing of a Friend's Onset of Alzheimer's

Not now, or tomorrow—
but some day. Each sunrise
and sunset in August gives up
a few minutes of summer

like the Himalayan vine, shriveling,
thorns following the cane

down to the pale
five-petal blossom, the stubborn fruit

ripening to blackberry.
How the tongue
relishes the taste.

M. Brett Gaffney, born in Houston, Texas, holds an MFA in poetry from Southern Illinois University Carbondale and is Art Editor of *Gingerbread House* literary magazine. Her poems have appeared or are forthcoming in *Exit 7, Still: the Journal, Permafrost, Scapegoat Review, Rogue Agent, museum americana, Devilfish Review, BlazeVOX, Fruita Pulp, Stirring, NonBinary Review, Sugared Water,* and *Zone 3,* among others. During the Halloween season she haunts the Dent School House in Cincinnati, Ohio where she lives with her partner and their dog, Ava.

Found

> *The body of Elisa Lam was found inside the water tank on the roof of the Cecil Hotel where it had been decomposing for 19 days.*

what is the taste of floating—
　　　　of our last moments—

when air is something we've forgotten
when a girl drowns in her tower

and we wait
for our bathtubs
　　　　to fill with night

Translator's Note

Li Shang-Yin was a student of the complex relations between men and women. His poems have drawn from folklore and legend as freely as from nature and his own experience. They have been driven by his unusually extensive use of allusion. These poems probably do not in every case record his own affairs and emotions, but the genuine passion and the unmistakable empathy in them suggest that he was deeply preoccupied with love, sexuality, and all the pleasures and pains that could arise in the course of infatuation, pursuit, loss and reconciliation.

Translating Li Shang-Yin's poems has been an exhilarating journey of feeling deeply humane, and seeing deeply into the mysteries of our common artistic existence. My translations are very much in line with the poet's qualities and passions.

Li-Shang Yin's (author, 813 – 858 late phase of the Tang) The late Tang Dynasty was an era marked by social turmoil and political uncertainty. Li-Shang Yin survived by attaching himself to government posts from librarian to sheriff to magistrate. His poems are allegories of his relations with his patrons, disguised accounts of his love-life, veiled political satires, or all at once. Though his political and economic fortunes fluctuated considerably, his literary reputation grew steadily. He became and has remained one of China's most admired and intriguing poets. The group of five poems called "Untitled" can be seen as central to his work.

Ann Yu Huang (translator) has poetry appearing online and in print extensively. Huang's first chapbook *Love Rhythms* was published by Finishing Line Press, a collection reviewed and noted by Orange County Metro. Her book-length collection of poems *White Sails* came out in Cherry Grove Imprints by WordTech Communications. To read or listen more about her poems, please visit www.byAnnHuang.com.

锦瑟

锦瑟无端五十弦，一弦一柱思华年。

庄生晓梦迷蝴蝶，望帝春心托杜鹃。

沧海月明珠有泪，蓝田日暖玉生烟。

此情可待成追忆，只是当时已惘然。

Zithern

Zithern with brilliant brocades
becomes endless with its fifty strings,
each string construes
a column that longs for its golden past.

Life is a dream well
intended, a docent named Hope is perplexed by a dream
of butterflies, an emperor named
Expectations lures after cuckoos.

Above the South Sea, the reflective moon is so
bright that makes pearls out of human tears.
Inflicted by the blue fields, a warm sun
smolders a piece of jade into mist.

Awaiting with remembrances,
the desolate feelings remain,
as if back then, time was only given
for the purpose of that moment.

重过圣女祠

白石岩扉碧藓滋，上清沦谪得归迟。
一春梦雨常飘瓦，尽日灵风不满旗。

萼绿华来无定所，杜兰香去未移时。

玉郎会此通仙籍，忆向天阶问紫芝。

Revisiting the Celestial Temple

The white cliff was dampened with jade
moss. There was this passage for the fallen
angels to exile and perish, through which they
had not wanted to return late.

Drizzling rains of Spring were
like floating tiles, surreal as the unopened
sailing flag by the end of the day and
magical winds continued blowing it.

The appearance of a goddess named Stem of Luscious
Flower could not be predictable for a conservative
statesman, a celestial child named Scent of Azalea
did not hesitate to leave her adoptive earthly father.

A young official who organized rankings for
the registry of the immortal kingdom queried, 'if
one desired to leave mortality behind, why
ignore the fairy grass for the very secret of youth?'

Jonathan Travelstead served in the Air Force National Guard for six years as a firefighter and currently works as a full-time firefighter for the city of Murphysboro. Having finished his MFA at Southern Illinois University of Carbondale, he now works on an old dirt-bike he hopes will one day get him to the salt flats of Bolivia. He has published work in *The Iowa Review* and on *Poetrydaily.com* among others, and his first collection *How We Bury Our Dead* by Cobalt/Thumbnail Press is forthcoming in February, 2015.

Analysis Paralysis

A quick in-and-out and nobody gets hurt,
you promise, looking at your watch
before walking with purpose
into the Kroger's. It's two-oh-five
and now you're standing before packaged meats
on Manager's Special, comparing orange
stickers on ground chuck for quantity
over quality, and so disregard
the usual systems used in judgement.
Marbling of fat, sodium levels, firmness
when pinched. Weigh your options among
the gray and the cast aside. Lean, cellophane-
wrapped burger two days shy of expiring.
The meat of this muscle's destiny
decided by arbitrary numbers
assigned if only to render slaughter
pointless. What time is it? Put the package
down to check your phone. Ten minutes,
you told yourself. Nine left, you
return to the lonely and the
rifled-through, preserved in their plastic-
and-styrofoam platters. Which were you holding?
This one- gray, nearly void of the red
dye injected for the illusion
of freshness. Drained,
you see it is sponged into the
foam backing with the tiny, diagonal
imprints on it, sandwiched between meat
and styrofoam. Holding the package
in your palms like an offering,
you press your thumbs,
squishing flesh to the side, realize
it's nothing more than an absorbent pad
for soaking up chemicals, what little blood
remains. You have second thoughts.
If you are what you eat
then you're either

the meat or what saturates
the pad. What time is it?
Exchange container
for one whose price's barcode
is digitally stamped on
the yellow tag. Three dollars for three-
point-eight-four pounds. Can that be right?
Weight, divided by cost- or cost
multiplied by net weight?
Pull out phone. Make necessary
calculations. See the icon for email.
So much spam. Thank you,
no, the penis pills
didn't work the first time. Pocket phone,
forget to check time and figure
for accuracy. Out.
Download app, but floaters
dance like amoeba across your
vision. Alphanumeric
symbols unwind,
hike across the label,
mountainous over beef.
A word said thirty
times loses its meaning's
hard edges, lies dumb
on the tongue.
Value. Isn't that what this
is about? How much it costs, living
this way. A magnetic pull as if on something
ferrous in your arm says check your
phone just as your mouth
starts forming exactly what the trade-off
for productivity is when the sprayers
and the muzak click on,
misting kale and broccoli to "Singing
in the Rain", and the voice
of Gene Kelly who says
Stand still, hotshot. You're not going
anywhere and you know he's right
because you're spread thin
over every perceived
possibility without action.
Eighty-percent of your energy
spent on a day's trivialities. It comes
like the forgotten arm in boxing
that you're in the corner
with a toothbrush when the dog's

dropped a deuce on the table,
a one-two that rises in
your stomach
to strike the sweet spot
in your head, that, though you
just looked, you still
don't know how long you've
been here, though it must be hours
more than the time usually
allotted for perusal
of discount meats. You know
you should just move on, but it's
like halon, or one of those chemicals
in fire extinguishers that
sucks the air right
out of your lungs, or a car
you're changing oil beneath that's
gone off its blocks, which now compresses
your chest like a night terror, the fear
fantasy that grips you while
driving where one of those stinger-
jacked truck drivers hurtling from the
coal mines on route three cream
your girlfriend-bedecked
scooter, or as you drive the two of you
out for Wednesday-night crab legs at Midland's
you suddenly remember what it was
that her Mother said,
and just as you turn to tell her
the body of a deer whose legs get swept out
from under it by your truck's bumper
hurtles through the front glass
and into the passenger seat
displacing her torso
from where she sits. All this
black and white tile. You can't breathe.
Even the cooler's cold air
is a thief skulking
the heat away.
You never insulated
yourself with contingency lists
you never made against anxiety, this
trouble you borrow against
an astronomical
monthly percentage rate.
So this is what it's like failing
gloriously at something,

though at what,
exactly, eludes you. Do we
have enough eggs? Cartons stretch, infinite,
down a hallway in your mind.
White ovals in their
recycled, corrugated glory as if
placed between mirrors you peer between,
see reflected forever. Thought.
What you're paralyzed by.
You don't know why you're here,
or what, if anything, is important anymore.
The volume cranks to eleven
on the muzak-
Who would do this to me?
but even as you ask, you know the answer.
Eyes retreat two inches into
their orbits. Your body,
exhausted by the mind still
dogging it. The sprayers go at it again,
and so does Gene Kelley, this
time cackling over
the chorus. People continue
to split, flow around your inaction
you protect with a sword flaming
at the Garden's gates.
What time is it?

Christine Kitano is the author of *Birds of Paradise*. The daughter of a Japanese American father and a Korean immigrant mother, she was born in Los Angeles. She teaches creative writing and Asian American literature at Ithaca College. Recent poems are published in *Tar River Poetry*, *Crab Orchard Review*, *Newfound Journal*, *Atticus Review*, and *Miramar*. For more information: http://www.chrisitnekitano.com.

Equinox
> Topaz Incarceration Camp, 1943

Blame the late storm.
Or blame the earth itself,
ice-stunned soil smothering
the torn green shoots.

Once another story, but now:
an empty house, an empty
field, an orchard emptying
of apples. At home so long,

then by dawn, we were gone.
This dawn: Utah's mountains
trimmed with a thin, purple
cold. But even this winter eases

into spring. Elsewhere,
water must rush forth.
Mist will clear, leaves will
brighten to green. With

or without permission,
another season will pass.
The fence leans its shadow,
but for how long

can one stand against
what the natural world
springs toward?

Chelsea Kindred is a fiction writer and international educator living in Texas. She received her MFA in Creative Writing from Chatham University where she was awarded the Best Thesis in Fiction. Her work has been published in *Corium Magazine*.

Circus

The circus then was peanut shells on dirty floors, hard plastic seats, the rich smell of elephant dung.

The circus then was cotton candy in my mouth, stuck to my fingers, in my sister's hair. The circus then was peeling white paint on the end of the clown's nose that squirted water from a daisy into my face.

The circus then was backs arched in the air, swinging from one bar to the next, floured hands catching invisible threads with a magic I couldn't comprehend.

The circus now is you sitting next to me, expecting me to be grateful for the expensive seats, the velvet plush, the cursive French *Cirque du Soleil* projected in light on the wall.

The circus now is wanting to forget the extra martini you had at dinner that made you mean, that made you pinch my ass, that took things too far by bringing up last week's argument at the grocery store.

The circus now is *will you slip will you fall will you miss it will your body untangle from the ribboned web will you catch will you connect will those arms be there to catch you when you fly through the air*

The circus now is dark, now is silent, now is frozen in fear as we watch the performer slip, just a second, just a twitch, and then her body is falling through space

arched

no bar to catch

no cotton candy

no fights in the grocery store

The circus now is body on floor, the circus now is bright lights on and every corner, every piece of floor is lit up, the circus now is the look of horror on your face, the way you look at me.

The circus now is over, the circus now is please leave, we've had an emergency. Please, look away.

KB Ballentine's work has appeared in numerous journals and publications, including *Alehouse, Tidal Basin Review*, and *Haight Ashbury Literary Journal*. A finalist for the 2014 Ron Rash Poetry Award, she was also a 2006 finalist for the Joy Harjo Poetry Award and was awarded the Dorothy Sargent Rosenberg Poetry Prize in 2006 and 2007. *Fragments of Light* (2009) and *Gathering Stones* (2008) were published by Celtic Cat Publishing. Her third collection, *What Comes of Waiting*, won the 2013 Blue Light Press Book Award.

Backscatter
Stroma, Scotland*

You remember only *Coinean*, the quilted bunny
stuffed with straw Mam replenished each summer,
ears droopy and soft, nose all but worn off.

Farmhouse sighs, wind hammering each broken board,
timber chopped and brought across the water
in *bátannach* too small for furniture.

Gannets and cormorants marble the rocks
with guano, scream as they skim eel grass
shifting in surf, fish scattering.

Light threads the splintered door. Outside,
buttercups beckon, waves crash against rock,
splash high — above you, the house.

Thistle sprouts in the collapsing kitchen.
And the spoon. It glints against soil,
rusts with briny air. You pick it up,

memory shining on the possibility of this:
oatmeal, warm and gleaming with honey,
a small fire, peat smoke earthy and salted,

small hands knitting a sock — laughter fading
from the room as sharp gusts shriek
around a corner of crumbling wall . . .

Fire evaporates with the sting of spray.
You are left to linger with relics of home
vanishing each day, reclaimed by wind and tide.

*Stroma is an abandoned island off the northeast coast of Scotland. The last residents left their island home in 1962. *The houses ... have rotted at different rates. Inside some ... everyday objects still remain where they were left decades ago.* —Bella Bathurst

Kirby Wright was the 2014 Writer in Residence at the Earthskin Artist Colony in Auckland, New Zealand. He wishes to dedicate "The Flute" to the memory of his mother.

The Flute

Waves break
the sands of Muriwai,
foam sliding up
the oily black coast.
Sea a milk glass blue.
A deserted beach,
The strand creating
Lonely and longing.
Takapu nest offshore,
On lava atolls
Angling like headstones.
The Tasman Sea rolls in
A spear of bamboo.
I accept this offering.
I saw, shape,
Carve holes in wood
Harder than bone.
Today I will
Walk the shore
Alone with the world
Blowing notes
From my flute
For the sea
And the birds.

Tom Holmes is the founding editor of *Redactions: Poetry, Poetics, & Prose*, and in July 2014, he also co-founded *RomComPom: A Journal of Romantic Comedy Poetry*. He is also author of seven collections of poetry, most recently *The Cave*, which won The Bitter Oleander Press Library of Poetry Book Award for 2013 and will be released in 2014. His writings about wine, poetry book reviews, and poetry can be found at his blog, *The Line Break*: *http://thelinebreak.wordpress.com/*.

Arctic Circle Cautioning (352 BCE)

If you travel north with urgency
past the last measurement
and through the speculations,

if you see atmosphere
non-distinct from geology
and ocean surface,

if you feel gelatinous,
shut quick your mouth
before it jumps and scurries off,

put your ear to the borealis,
curl your fingers into canoes,
hold your breath, and burrow.

The North will melt. You will float
home – the home pockmarked by salt
and pressure from a deepening sea.

Jacqueline Haskins is a biologist of watery wilds, from cypress swamps to cirque swales. She has received a Pushcart nomination and been a finalist in *Oregon Quarterly's* Northwest Perspectives Contest. Her work appears in *The Iowa Review, River Teeth Journal, Raven Chronicles,* and elsewhere. Stop by and say hello at JacquelineHaskins.com.

Three Little Uglies

Cherry Creek, 1967

That smell. Not floating petals, not spun vanilla-ice. Our Cherry Creek smelled fevery, green-brown, rotten on the edges. It smelled like deception. Us two kids staring into the edgeless shadows behind water spilling over a sand-wedged log; the water fell long and straight as my sister's hair, then curled under itself into dank black. Our first glimpse of infinity. Cherry Creek smelled weedy, like abandonment. It smelled free, not just of time, but of all the ignorance of adulthood.

Airport Inn, 2012

In the cramped basement, noise splatters off the walls, drowning my brain in racket. The pool is a postage stamp. Scuzzy water sloshes over the cheap tiles and across our feet— two grumpy grownups marooned in plastic chairs—then sucks back into the pool again.

"Go!" The boys leap into the air. "Cannonball!" Another tsunami.

They clamber out, laughter racking Noah like a coughing fit. "Again!"

The clamshell room stinks with chlorine and sanitizer, clamors hard cleanable surfaces. We don't open the tiny window because tires roll past at eye level, idling cars exhaling against the glass. Er, plastic. Airplanes shriek overhead. Yes, it was the prince of internet deals.

It's quieter the next day, in the car: just three boys talking at once.

I turn toward the back seat. "So what was your favorite part of the whole trip?"

I wonder if they'll say the Science Center's grand finale, giant colored bubbles floating up from the stage, then flashing into flame with a blazing whumpf. Or maybe Pike Place Market, google-eyed dead fish at eye level, drummers, jugglers, the street magician who shows us a red ace, hands Noah a red ace, Noah opens his hand—the ace is black. Perhaps rolling down Gasworks Park's long grassy hill at sunset. Or the gag gifts they're bringing home from Archie McPhee's—gelatinous brains, underpants for squirrels, and a nose-shaped pencil sharpener (insert pencil into nostril...)

Nope. Instant and unanimous. "The swimming pool!"

Cherry Creek, 1967

I had to grow up to notice what an ugly little creek it was. A gully. Cut down— *way* down it seemed to us then—below street level. Below, mysterious, apart.

But also right there, right across the street from suburban lawns. Mangy cottonwoods stood sentry. We passed between them, scrambling down a steep prickly hill. Today it might be a refuge for the homeless or a place to shoot up. Back in our world, a place we could invent each time, a scrap of freedom.

From the creek, across a *big* street—with a yellow line and everything—was the reservoir. Shaped like the bowl of a spoon, Shallow-edged, mud-bottomed, Cherry Creek Reservoir was ringed with asphalt, goose shit, and mowed grass, slick and trampled. Moms dangling bags of Wonderbread towered like cottonwoods; toddlers clutched crusts, flapping. The ducks, mostly farmyard white, swirled like a wake of white froth. White people went around and around, carousel-like, on the black asphalt loop. At the reservoir, everyone was on display, everything under control.

Which is why we always went the other way, sneaker-skidding down, down to the creek. Did anyone else even know about it? Did it exist only for us?

Meadowlark Development, 2015

Redwing blackbirds careen and bray; cottonwood fluff falters. *Forever young*, the redwings shout, a disorganized chorus of Bob Dylans. Do you think they know the days will get hotter, the water sag and cloud, oozier, scummier; the cattail cobs darken and puff off into the wind? Are they shouting to the bulldozers, standing by, ready to break ground for affordable housing?The plan is to suck all this wet stuff into a pipe, and bury it under affordable asphalt.

Over in erudite Seattle, they're daylighting little buried streams. Maybe not in the low-income neighborhoods.

This affordable field, left empty while houses sprouted up across the street, has long been riddled with wet. The previous owner will walk it with you, point out drains and pipes he, his Dad, his grandpa installed. This affordable field is where the deer, drowsing out the afternoon in the tall grass on the shady side of Rattlesnake Hill, slip down in the evening to drink. Where coyote tracks powder the ground in winter. Where a beaver skull lay lodged in mud beneath the cattails. A lady-slipper orchid, and snowy-shy triangles of trillium, bloom beside survey stakes. Orange flagging snaps in the wind. On a stake slashed by black writing, a redwing blackbird perches to sing of love. Or maybe infinity. Or maybe he sings: *everything here is mine.*

Can't we build this fifteen acre development and also save this bit of wet? Dear city administrator. Dear mayor. Dear councilmembers. Dear Department of Ecology. Dear Army Corps of Engineers. *That's just an irrigation ditch, they shrug.Actually, no,* I take a breath, *it's more complicated.* I start to tell about the old landowner, his grandfather, the drains and tiles, the orchid, the redwings, keep surface water on the surface, I say, but look, their eyes are wandering. There is so much to attend to in this world. Polar ice caps are melting. They thank me for my time.

The comment period closes neatly as a reservoir's asphalt loop. That's it. Turn's over. I hesitate, one foot pointed toward realism. Or …cowardice? People chain themselves to redwoods, but...weedy irrigation ditches?

On the edge of the field, the bulldozers catnap, sleepy lions.

Cherry Creek

Do you remember the press of sun-soaked sand in the arches of your feet?

Cherry Creek, our place. Synonymous with us. We were safe there, in a way we carried inside. A way we had no idea could be lost.

We shed shoes and socks and pants and rules and grownups. Hours unswirled like bubbles underwater. Time turned back around itself as we dug the snake's tail into its mouth, as we dug endless meandering mazes riddled with moats and ponds.

We leapt, rock to underwater rock, scum slick beneath our toes. We were hunters, at Cherry Creek. The air smelled dangerous, like slime. Giants, we threw our shadows across darting fish. Masters of a tangled universe, we waded in a rot-stained ribbon, time.

My sister could scoop the quicksilver fish in her hands. We put them into the mazes plowed by our bulldozer fists. Our prisoners.

Love, infinity, mine. Life, in water, over glinting sand. A mystery, a black ace, we kept turning in our hands.

Rajiv Mohabir received the 2014 Intro Prize in Poetry by Four Way Books for his first full-length collection *The Taxidermist's Cut* (Spring 2016), the 2015 AWP Intro Journal Award, the Kundiman Prize for *The Cowherd's Son*, and a PEN/Heim Translation Fund Grant. His fellowships Voices of Our Nation's Artist foundation, Kundiman, and the American Institute of Indian Studies language program. His poetry and translations are internationally published or forthcoming from journals such as *Best American Poetry 2015, Quarterly West, Guernica, Prairie Schooner, Crab Orchard Review, Drunken Boat, Anti-, Great River Review, PANK,* and *Aufgabe*. He received his MFA in Poetry and Translation from at Queens College, CUNY where he was Editor in Chief of the Ozone Park Literary Journal. Currently he is pursuing a PhD in English from the University of Hawai`i, where he teaches poetry and composition.

Burst

Crack the crest
of the ocean face. Suck in air
and blow out

drops caught in your rostrum's V.

Remember the flare
of an algal bloom,
relics in this world of poison and oil

that glaze the sea
into arc-light, the brine crowned with horns

to gore us into loss'
bright shaft.

Goodbye for the Season

All afternoon white caps
hat trick the blue.
I imagine a whale spouts

across the sea's gem-face, sun
glints and our backs
face *mauka*

ironwood needles and *ti* leaves
sing rain songs.

Every year they return to
and leave Mokule'ia;

the lava rocks recall
fire now quelled.

Now they are empty.
I look back and you are
a word I've forgotten;

so many giants now ghosts.

Meiko Ko is a Singaporean living in New York. She is working to become a writer and a prose poet, and she attends the Second Saturdays Reading Series every month. She's published in *SoftBlow Magazine* and *Singapore Poetry*.

Goodbye

Once I didn't believe I was a person, I didn't insist it, I didn't insist on the breasts bound to my body or the riot in my womb, and this was wrong. This was wrong because I met a man on a stairwell. He was climbing down the stairs of a HDB flat as I was climbing up, and we were in each other's way. I moved to my right to let him pass but he was like a mirror he moved to his right, then it was as though we were saying yes and no at the same time we both moved to our lefts. The sky above the parapet wall was greying, and in its grey was a wind carrying the cries of sparrows. The man began to smile as he pointed to the sky, it was a smile borne on a wind, it was a smile crying with sparrows. A clock was moving ahead and at seven pm there was a flicker and the flat lighted up, the fluorescence was like water around us, and I grew shy of the man's smile. He turned sideways to let me pass, and with my eyes lowered I walked past him and up the flight of steps. When I turned back I saw him waving goodbye. It was a goodbye layered by white light, it was the shadow of a right arm resting on the floor of the stairwell.

2014 & 2015 Contest Results

2015 Contest: Short-ish Poems (under 42 lines)

Judge: Sheryl St. Germain
Readers: Jennifer Jackson Berry, Jillian Phillips, Marissa Schwalm, **Sarah Winn**

Winner: Monic Ductan's "How to be Massaged by a Man you Think you No Longer Love"
Runner:Up: Michaelle Gaffney's "Found"

Semi-Finalists (in alphabetical order) –
Kelli Allen's "Market Day in Someone Else's City"
Carol Bachofner's "Hipster, Gangster, Poet"
Michaelle Gaffney's "The Pack"
Lizzi Wolf's "Blue Frog"

2015 Contest: Longish Poems (100-200 lines)
Judge: Jeffrey Schultz
Readers: Natalie Christine Mattila, **Ron Salutsky**
Winner: Jed Myers' "Movie Day"
Runner: Up: withdrawn

Semi-Finalists (in alphabetical order) –
Kevin Clark's "Aunt Rosas Idea"
Kelly McQuain's "Artery"
Judith Skillman's "Kingdom Come"

Blue Lyra Review's second round of contests was held during the month of April 2015.

We are also pleased to announce the winners to our previous 2014 contests (omitted in last print issue):

Blue Lyra Review's Short Poem Contest (under 65 lines)

Judge: Katherine Young

Winner: Mobi Warren's "Sesame Seeds Pray" (published in 2014 print issue)
Runner up: Gail Goepfert's "Revivify" (published online in Spring 2015)

Semi-Finalists (in alphabetical order)—
Gail Goepfert's "Suture"
Mobi Warren's "Papel Picado"

Blue Lyra Review's Flash Fiction Contest

Judge: Stefanie Freelie

Winner: William Hawkins' "Picking Up Zoos" (published in 2014 print issue)
Runner Up: Gordon Ball's "The Breaking" (published online in Spring 2015)

Semi-Finalists (in alphabetical order)—
James Clark's "Wexler's Car"
Bernard Grant's "Wind"
Emily Kiernan's "White Sands, 1945"
Renee Thompson's "Recovery"
Preeva Tramiel's "The Driving Lesson"

Blue Lyra Review's Living Earth Nonfiction Prize

Judge: Apt Russell

Winner: Julie Jeanell Leung's "Reclamation" (published in 2014 print issue)
Runner Up: Chelsey Clammer's "I Live in a Town" (online in Spring 2015)

Semi-Finalists (in alphabetical order)—
Wendy Fontaine's "Sand Dollars"
Jessamyn Smith's "The White Deer"

Blue Lyra Review's Longish Poem Prize (100-200 lines)

Judge: Andrew Mcfadyen-Ketchum

Winner: Susanna Lang's "The Long Way Back" (published in print issue 2014)
Runner-Up: David Kann's "The Language of the Farm" (online in Spring 2015)

Semi-Finalists (in alphabetical)—
Janet Joyner's "Women's History Week"
Lucian Mattison's "Circumambient"
Arthur Plotnik's "On the Beach at Nazare"
Lauren Rusk's "Lessons"
Chris Warner's "The New Math"
Jeremy Windham's "Look to the Little Dipper"

The previous contest readers from 2014 (who we are super grateful for) include:

Ann Beman
Michelle Brafman
Brittany D. Clark
Risa Denenberg
Donelle Dreese
Anthony Frame
Iris Graville
Brett Elizabeth Jenkins
Kelly Miller
Lauren Michele Plitkins
Nichole L. Reber
Nomi Stone
Annaliese Wagner

Calazaza's Delicious Dereliction

Poems by **Suzanne Dracius**
Translated by **Nancy Naomi Carlson**
November 1, 2015
Pages 130, $16.95
ISBN: 978-1-936797-64-6
Available now at tupelopress.org or contact
orders@tupelopress.org.

"We are indebted to Nancy Naomi Carlson who transported
these verses into English with verve and piquancy, aural skill
and consummate knowledge. We should give high praise to
this expert translation of a formidable poet."
— Orlando Ricardo Menes

In her polyphonic poems, Suzanne Dracius creates
protagonists—usually *calazazas*, light-skinned mulatto women
with red or blond hair—who fight like Amazons
against racial and gender discrimination. Dracius's voice is
leaping and exalted, often sexually charged, and infused with
allusions to Greek and Roman mythology.

www.ingramcontent.com/pod-product-compliance
Lightning Source LLC
Chambersburg PA
CBHW071200130626
46555CB00004B/1530

* 9 780692 619728 *